Current Approaches

Fibre – Is It Good For You?

Edited by
V Marks & N Goeting

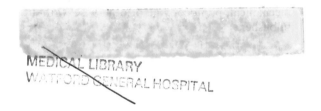

duphar
medical relations

First published 1990

ISBN 1–870678–23–0

Printed in Great Britain by
Henry Ling Ltd., at the Dorset Press, Dorchester, Dorset

CONTENTS

FOREWORD

The emotional response engendered by the term 'dietary fibre' is very different from that aroused by 'roughage'—the name by which dietary fibre was largely known prior to the 'healthy eating' boom which began in the mid-1970s with the appearance of a number of 'consensus reports'. What such reports lacked in factual evidence they made up for in enthusiasm and advocacy. One of the overwhelming messages they conveyed was that lack of dietary fibre is a major cause of numerous illnesses collectively and incorrectly called 'the diseases of affluence'. Included in the list are such diverse nosological entities as colon cancer, cholelithiasis, diabetes mellitus, atherosclerosis, diverticulitis and obesity, not to mention constipation or 'the English disease'.

Although an attractive idea, the concept of dietary fibre as an essential constituent of the human diet on a par with proteins, essential fatty acids and vitamins, has little basis in fact and as the contributors to this volume show, the current widely held view that a diet high in 'dietary fibre' is necessarily a good one, is far from established. Indeed, the very idea that there is any uniformity in dietary fibre is shown to be incorrect and, when used in this unqualified way, the term is pretty near to being meaningless.

Several different classes of chemical entities having in common only the fact that they are all complex polysaccharides of plant origin constitute what is collectively known as 'dietary fibre'. They exert a role in human nutrition partly by virtue of their chemical nature and partly by their topographical relationship to the other constituents of the foods within which they are contained. Both of these properties of diverse types of 'dietary fibre' are considered by our contributors, all of whom have personal research, and often experimental, experience of the subject on which they have been invited to write. This short volume, which is the product of a conference on Fibre held at the Royal College of Physicians under the auspices of Duphar Medical Relations will, I hope, make a useful and informed contribution to the continuing debate on the proper role of 'dietary fibre' in human nutrition.

VINCENT MARKS, MA, DM, FRCP, FRCPath
Professor of Clinical Biochemistry

EXPLODING THE MYTH OF FIBRE

B Moran

Clinician/Research Fellow

Southampton General Hospital

Fibre is a non-specific but useful term for any non-starch polysaccharide which is not degraded by human intestinal enzymes. The main site of action of fibre is at the level of the colon. Thus the main mechanism of action must involve an effect on colonic function.

In looking at the function of fibre we must therefore look at the functions of the human colon. The general perception of colonic function is that the colon is a residue for waste matter and that it absorbs water and electrolytes. Physicians and surgeons have long been interested in colonic function, particularly in failure of the colon to evacuate i.e. constipation. Goodhart[1] stated 'I have known the happiness of a whole household to hang daily on the regularity of an old man's bowels'. Thus the problem of constipation is not a new one and colonic function or dysfunction may well have far-reaching effects!

Many had noted the effect of bran in the treatment of constipation and by 1936 Dimock[2] was able to review 50 papers reporting clinical, biochemical, radiological and physiological studies of the use of fibre in constipation. He concluded that 'bran exerts a mechanical laxative action due to its fibre content, retaining moisture and allowing all the residues of the colon to resist dehydration'.

However it was only in the late 1960's and early 1970's that the 'fibre revolution' really gathered momentum. Based mainly on epidemiological observations on the prevalence of disease in Western society and in the Third World, Burkitt proposed that much of Western disease was related to a lack of dietary fibre.[3,4,5,6]

There is little doubt that Burkitts previous clinical and epidemiological observations on children with peculiar tumours, the so-called 'Burkitts lymphoma' were, and still are, a major landmark in the history of medicine. The fact that a virus could be implicated in the aetiology of a malignancy, and that this cancer was eminently treatable with chemotherapy, was a major advance in the field of human cancer. These observations begged the question—Could fibre be the answer to many of the diseases of the Western World? There were many who thought it might and a book entitled 'F-plan diet'[7] was a best-seller in 1982 and has remained popular since then. The proposals were that a diet high in fibre or 'roughage' was not only the best method to lose weight but could also influence health and happiness.

However it must be stated that at this time there was evidence that fibre was useful in the treatment of certain diseases, such as diverticular disease.[8] Fibre was noted to alter intestinal transit time and increase stool weight,[9] but the

1

central theme was that fibre was a bulking agent, acted as a water retaining sponge and resulted in bigger stools. Bigger stools were in some way better for you!

It then became apparent that there might be different types of fibre and when Stephen and Cummings[10] compared cabbage and bran fibre in equal doses they found that 10% of cabbage fibre was recovered in the stools compared with 60% of bran fibre. This implied that fibre could be fermented in the colon by the resident flora and that some fibre was more digestible than others. These authors also compared the bacterial mass when control subjects took additional fibre. Cabbage and carrot produced a large increase in bacterial mass (from 15 g bacteria to 19 g/day) and bran produced a smaller response (15 to 17 g/day). It would appear that fermentable or so-called 'digestible' fibre results in a proliferation of bacterial mass with a relationship between the amount fermented and the increase in bacterial mass.

Thus some of the myths of fibre began to be dispelled: fibre is not 'indigestible' as shown by the disappearance of 90% of cabbage fibre. Furthermore fibre is not merely a 'bulking' agent but has been shown to be a modulator of bacterial activity in the colon. When you consider that the number of colonic bacteria outnumbers the cells in the body[11] this has major metabolic implications.

FIBRE AND COLONIC FUNCTION

There are problems in understanding the effect of fibre on colonic function because of limited knowledge of that function and also the methods which have been used to obtain information. The importance of the colonic flora has already been mentioned and if we look at the colonic flora in liver disease we see that a paradox exists: do we give antibiotics, such as neomycin, and kill the flora or do we feed them with a non-digestible polysaccharide such as lactulose? In clinical practise we use both treatments in combination[12] and nobody really knows how these antagonistic treatments work.

To demonstrate how limited our knowledge of colonic function is I will explore a myth surrounding colonic function which our research has allowed us to dispel. We have a particular interest in nitrogen metabolism, particularly the metabolism of urea which is the main end-product of human nitrogen metabolism. The original concept, based on nitrogen balance techniques, was that on a normal intake of nitrogen the major daily loss from the body was in the urine and that the 1 g of stool nitrogen represented unabsorbed dietary nitrogen. However with the development of nitrogen labelling techniques it was noted that protein turnover was of the order of 40–50 g nitrogen daily i.e. four to five times the daily intake or loss of nitrogen. Of more relevance to colonic function was the finding that there was a large movement of nitrogen into and out of the lower bowel daily such that the 1 g faecal nitrogen was the result of a considerable metabolic activity.

This movement of nitrogen has been quantified[13] as of the order of 15 g entering the bowel with 14 g being reabsorbed. Approximately one fifth (i.e. 3 g/day) of this nitrogen is urea nitrogen and is hydrolysed into ammonia by the intestinal flora. Urea has been found to be a good marker of this movement of nitrogen in the lower bowel.[13] It is therefore of relevance to examine some aspects of urea metabolism. On a normal intake of 11 g nitrogen approximately 9 g of urea nitrogen is formed in the liver. It is now accepted that 30% of this urea (about 3 g urea nitrogen) is broken down in the body[14] and that this is a function of the intestinal bacteria.[15]

By far and away the majority of the intestinal bacteria in man are confined to the colon[11] and so it has been generally accepted that the hydrolysis of urea is mainly a function of the colonic flora. If you give antibiotics effective against the colonic flora you can dramatically reduce this hydrolysis.[15] The major controversy arises as to how the urea gets to the flora as very little enters from the ileum.[16] This study was in ileostomy subjects but has since been confirmed by direct sampling using long intestinal tubes.[17] All this evidence points towards urea crossing the colonic wall. However previous investigators have concluded that the colon is virtually impermeable to urea.[18,19] We reasoned that if the colon is impermeable to urea, then it is impossible to explain either the mechanism or the site of the known urea hydrolysis.

We looked at how these investigators had studied colonic permeability. Wolpert and colleagues[18] used the so-called 'oro caecal intubation' method. A long tube is passed through the small intestine into the colon, the colon is washed out and cleansed completely of its contents and a urinary catheter is then placed in the rectum and the balloon inflated. The solution in question is then perfused through the colon and the effluent is sampled. This method is the basis for much of the work on colonic function and has indeed provided us with some useful figures such as that the colon can absorb 5700 mls of water per day, 814 meq sodium and 44 meq potassium.[20]

Similarly Bown and colleagues[21] used perfusion studies of the excluded colon and found similar results with regard to water and electrolyte absorption. The excluded colon resulted from an operation performed in the 60's in patients suffering from recurrent hepatic encephalopathy. It was thought that by excluding the colon and anastomosing the caecum to the rectum, you could prevent hepatic encephalopathy. The colon was brought out as two colostomies leaving an excluded defunctioned colon. This operation has been abandoned as the post-operative mortality was high and encephalopathy was not prevented. However, it was a convenient model for the study of colonic function, in that it was possible to intubate the proximal and distal stomata and perfuse a solution through the colon.

Perfusion of urea solutions through the intact colon, following oro-caecal intubation[18] and through the excluded colon[19] provided similar results and suggested that the colon was virtually impermeable to urea.

However the normal colonic transit time is of the order of 40–60 hours[22] and normal intestinal contents have been shown to enhance intestinal permeability.[23] Furthermore, if you extrapolate the perfusion rate of 10 mls/min to 24 hours you get a figure of 14.4 litres per day. This evidence suggests that perfusion studies are unlikely to represent colonic function.

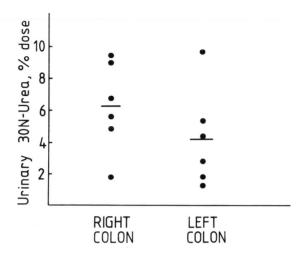

Figure 1. The recovery of 30N-urea as a percentage of the dose instilled into the right and left colon via the biopsy channel of the colonoscope.

We decided to evaluate colonic permeability from a different viewpoint using stable isotope labelled nitrogen. Nitrogen exists in three atomic weights, 13N or radio-active nitrogen, 14N the commonly occurring atomic form and 15N or the stable isotope of nitrogen. The half-life of 13N is too short for any meaningful studies of nitrogen metabolism and it is of course radioactive and therefore has potential risks in human subjects. For these reasons studies of nitrogen and protein metabolism are generally confined to the use of 15N labelling techniques using a mass spectrometer to analyse the samples. It is possible to label both nitrogens of urea with 15N to give 15N15N-urea or 30N-urea. Double labelled urea placed in the lumen of the colon can have one of three fates; it may be excreted in the stool; it may be absorbed intact and excreted as urinary 30N-urea or luminal urea may be hydrolysed and absorbed as ammonia, reformed into urea in the liver and excreted as urinary 29N-urea.

For the purposes of the present argument we will confine ourselves to the urinary recovery of labelled urea. In our initial studies we placed a tracer dose of 30N-urea (1.5 mg/kg) in the lumen of the colon, via the biopsy channel of the colonoscope, and analysed the urine.[24] We placed the isotope in the caecum in six subjects and distal to the splenic flexure in six. The recovery of 30N-urea is outlined in Figure 1. We could recover 30N-urea in all subjects but the % recovery was low. We reasoned that this was due to rapid intraluminal urea hydrolysis by the colonic flora and we looked for a model of colonic function in which the colonic flora was likely to be reduced. One such model is patients with a so called 'defunctioning' or loop colostomy. The faecal stream exits from the right colon and the left colon is defunctioned. In separate studies we intubated the right and left stomata in five patients, injected the label into

4

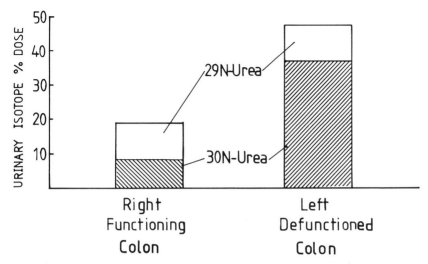

Figure 2. The median recovery, as a percentage of the dose of 30N-urea instilled into the right functioning colon and the left defunctioned colon, via the stomata of a defunctioning colostomy in separate studies in five patients. The median recovery as 30N-urea (urea absorbed intact) is significantly greater from the defunctioned colon ($P<0.01$, Wilcoxon rank sum). There was little difference in the recovery of label as 29N-urea (urea hydrolysed into ammonia and reformed into urea in the liver).

the lumen and analysed the urine for labelled urea. The results are outlined in Figure 2.

All subjects had a proportion of the dose of 30N-urea in the urine. There were significant differences between the defunctioned and the functioning colon ($P<0.01$, Wilcoxon rank sum). We then considered that the left colon may behave in a different manner from the right colon. We therefore recruited 5 patients with a left sided end-colostomy to study the left functioning colon. The recovery of labelled urea from the left defunctioned and the left functioning colon is shown in Figure 3. The recovery of 30N-urea is significantly different ($P<0.01$, Wilcoxon rank sum).

Taking into account that the defunctioned human colon has been shown to have markedly reduced absorptive capacity[25] our results suggest that the colon is readily permeable to urea. The difficulty in demonstrating this may have been due in part to the methods by which the colon was studied and in part to the rapid hydrolysis of available urea. The unequivocal demonstration of colonic permeability to urea would suggest that colonic perfusion studies must be interpreted with great caution and may, in some areas, be inaccurate.

The colon plays a major part in nitrogen and protein metabolism in man. This metabolism is a function of the colonic flora and a major role of fibre is as a substrate for this intense metabolic activity. It is of interest that one of the

5

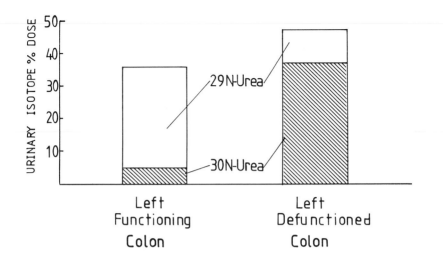

Left
Functioning
Colon

Left
Defunctioned
Colon

Figure 3. The median recovery (% of the dose) following instillation of 30N-urea into the functioning left colon in five subjects compared to the recovery from the defunctioned colon in the subjects with a defunctioning colostomy. Recovery as 30N-urea was significantly different ($P < 0.01$ Wilcoxon rank sum). A greater proportion of the dose was recovered as 29N-urea from the functioning colon, though the difference was not statistically significant.

consistent effects of fibre is an increase in stool nitrogen with a corresponding decrease in stool ammonia.[10]

Fibre may certainly have many beneficial functions and is not merely a bulking agent. Many of the myths that surround fibre are due to myths surrounding colonic function. The colon, with its flora, is an important metabolic organ and warrants more detailed investigation.

REFERENCES

1 Goodhart J F. Round about constipation. *Lancet* 1902;**ii**:1241.
2 Dimock E M. Treatment of habitual constipation by the bran method. MD Thesis; Cambridge: 1936.
3 Burkitt D P. Related disease-related cause. *Lancet* 1969;**ii**:1229.
4 Burkitt D P. The aetiology of appendicitis. *Br J Surg* 1971a;**58**:595.
5 Burkitt D P. Epidemiology of cancer of the colon and rectum. *Cancer* 1971b;**28**:3.
6 Burkitt D P. Varicose veins, deep vein thrombosis and haemorrhoids: Epidemiology and suggested aetiology. *Br Med J* 1972;**2**:556.
7 Eyton A. F-plan diet. Middlesex; Penguin Books: 1982.
8 Painter N S, Almeida A L, Cloebourne K W. Unprocessed bran in the treatment of diverticular disease of the colon. *Br Med J* 1972;**2**:137.

9 Burkitt D P, Walker A R P, Painter N S. Effect of dietary fibre on stools and transit time and its role in the causation of disease. *Lancet* 1972;**ii**:1408.

10 Stephen A M, Cummings J H. Mechanism of action of dietary fibre in the human colon. *Nature* 1980;**284**:283.

11 Gustafsson B E. The physiological importance of the colonic microflora. *Scand J Gastroenterol* 1982;**S77**:117–31.

12 Schafer D F. In hepatic coma the problem comes from the colon, but will the answers come from there? *J Lab Clin Med* 1987;**110**:253–4.

13 Jackson A A, Picou D, Landman J. The non-invasive measurement of urea kinetics in normal man by a constant infusion of 15N15N-urea. *Hum Nutr Clin Nutr* 1984;**38**:339–54.

14 Walser M, Bodenlos L J. Urea metabolism in man. *J Clin Invest* 1959;**38**:1617–26.

15 Richards P. Nutritional potential of nitrogen recycling in man. *Am J Clin Nutr* 1972;**25**:615–25.

16 Gibson J A, Park N J, Sladen G E, Dawson A M. The role of the colon in urea metabolism in man. *Clin Sci Mol Med* 1976;**50**:51–9.

17 Chadwick V S, Jones J D, Debongnie J C *et al*. Urea, uric acid and creatinine fluxes through the small intestine in man. *Gut* 1977;**18**:A944.

18 Wolpert E, Phillips S F, Summerskill W H J. Transport of urea and ammonia production in the human colon. *Lancet* 1971;**ii**:1387–90.

19 Bown R L, Gibson J A, Fenton J C B *et al*. Ammonia and urea transport by the excluded human colon. *Clin Sci Mol Med* 1975;**48**:279–87.

20 Devroede G H, Phillips S F. Conservation of sodium chloride and water by the human colon. *Gastroenterology* 1969;**56**:101–9.

21 Bown R L, Gibson G E, Rousseau B *et al*. A study of water and electrolyte transport by the excluded human colon. *Clin Sci* 1972;**43**:891–902.

22 Cummings J H. Constipation, dietary fibre and the control of large bowel function. *Postgraduate Med J* 1984;**60**:811–19.

23 Houpt T R, Houpt K A. Transfer of urea nitrogen across the rumen wall. *Am J Physiol* 1968;**214**:1296–1303.

24 Moran B J, Jackson A A. 15N-urea metabolism in the human colon: evidence for intraluminal hydrolysis and mucosal permeability. *Gut* 1990 (in press).

25 Roediger W E W. Bacterial short-chain fatty acids and mucosal diseases of the colon. *Br J Surg* 1988;**75**:346–8.

DISCUSSION

Audience   You mentioned that the faecal nitrogen losses go up in people taking fibre. If someone was in a precarious nitrogen balance, would this increase in faecal nitrogen loss throw them into negative balance or is the nitrogen that would come out in the faeces non utilisable nitrogen?

Mr Moran   Our evidence would suggest that the nitrogen which comes out in the faeces is taken from urea nitrogen, so the main mechanism for the control of nitrogen balance in man is through alterations in the production and excretion of urea. If your stool nitrogen is increased, urea nitrogen, or nitrogen in the urine, tends to be diminished. The balance is just shifted from urinary nitrogen to stool nitrogen, as has been documented in some studies.

Prof Marks Presumably there is also increasing bacterial bulk and therefore some of that nitrogen is bacterial protein nitrogen.

Mr Moran Yes. Cummings demonstrated increased bacterial nitrogen by isolation of bacteria. Also bacteria contain a lot of water; probably one of the mechanisms by which stool weight is increased.

Prof Marks One of the rationales in using lactulose for hepatic encephal-opathy is that you change the pH of colonic contents and so keep the ammonia that would otherwise be traipsing around, within the colon. Is there any evidence for that theory of increased acidity of colonic contents?

Mr Moran We would suggest that it is not as simple as an alteration in pH and I think the recent studies would confirm that. It is a simplistic view that there are good bugs and bad bugs, and that the good bugs eat up the ammonia and retain it and the bad bugs produce too much ammonia, which is then absorbed. This view would of course explain why neomycin kills off the bad ones and lactulose feeds the good ones. However, there certainly are alterations in bacterial metabolism.

Dr Eastwood You talked about colonic permeability. We know that this varies under a number of circumstances, for example in ileal resection, where there is an enhanced flow of bile acids into the colon, oxylate permeability alters. Do you have evidence in relation to luminal pH or nitrogen content that there is any change in colonic permeability, for example based on polyethelene glycol and measurements of pore size?

Mr Moran We have been interested in nitrogen metabolism around the colon and have not actually looked at permeability to other molecules. We reasoned that previous findings just could not fit with what goes on in human metabolism, and based our investigations and findings on this. The problem with the colon is that it is a very inaccessible organ and so one of the least investigated. However, the recent introduction and widespread use of the colonoscope has helped to elucidate some of the problems with colonic function.

Prof Bloom Have there been any attempts to distinguish the effects of pH and the effects of carbohydrate metabolism by, for example, acidifying colonic contents with buffers or resins that can be taken orally?

Mr Moran I think if you take buffers orally the majority would be absorbed, but we have not actually investigated the colonic pH as a separate entity.

Prof Bloom Prof Marks has suggested that pH may be one of the mechan-isms by which things act. It is indistinguishable from the effects of carbo-hydrate metabolism which might be much more potent, so that the importance of colonic pH may be a myth.

Mr Moran   It is difficult to get at the normal colon. We readily admit that our models of colonic function are not the normal colon, but approximations. All studies start from a background in which what happens in the colon is not really known. To find out we have to put tubes down from the mouth, and do all sorts of things which are not physiological. So, I am not very familiar with the work done on colonic pH since we have not involved ourselves in that area.

EPIDEMIOLOGY—THE STORY SO FAR

Professor D J P Barker

Director

MRC Environmental Epidemiology Unit

University of Southampton

This paper will discuss appendicitis because the study of this disease gave rise to the idea that the absence of fibre in the diet might be a major predisposing factor in diseases which are collectively known as 'Western diseases'.

In 1920 Professor Rendle Short[1] studied the rise of appendicitis which had occurred in Britain in the previous 20 years and concluded that this was a result of the relatively lower quantity of cellulose which was being eaten because of wider use of imported foods. This was the origin of the fibre hypothesis in relation to 'Western diseases'. Subsequent events were described by Robert Graves in 'The Long Weekend'. In 1927 the Lancet introduced the idea of 'roughage', stating that it was useless to eat nothing but vitamins, proteins and carbohydrates. These needed something fibrous to introduce them to the intestine. Thus 'Roughage' was the last term to enter the popular dietetic vocabulary. It was interpreted to mean something scratchy like bran, the peel that had previously been removed from stringy celery and the stalky ends of asparagus—all of which should facilitate utilisation of vitamins. 'Roughage' breakfast foods such as bran became available to supply this need. Bran, which had been removed from flour in order to give the bleached appearance of white bread that people liked was now being sold back to them in packets costing as much as 3 small loaves.

Had Rendle Short known what would happen to appendicitis in the next 60 years he probably would not have come to his original conclusion. Figure 1 is a graph of the changes in mortality from appendicitis from 1901 to 1980 in England and Wales, on a logarithmic scale.[2] The literature on appendicitis in this country is so rich that one can be confident that the changes shown here, that is: a rise, a plateau and a decline, mirror changes in the actual occurrence of the disease. From 1901 onwards there was a steep rise in appendicitis in Britain, as there was in other European countries. The incidence of appendicitis reached a plateau in the inter-war years, and thereafter declined. In Figure 1 the decline appears to begin around 1940, but if the age-specific trends are examined, it is clear that appendicitis rates were falling from the middle of the 1930s in all age groups except the very old. This group are an exception because they have a very low occurrence of the disease, but dominate the all ages mortality picture because case fatality is high. The decline in appendicitis rate since the 1930s was unaffected by changes in diet which occurred during the war; and since the war there has been continuous and progressive decline. This is not an artefact, but can be seen in hospital surveys, general practice consultations and national hospital statistics. It is a phenomenon which has

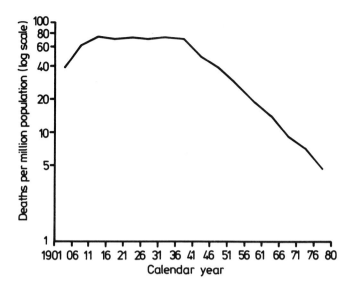

Figure 1. Average annual mortality rates for appendicitis in both sexes combined 1901–80, England and Wales.[2]

also occurred in North America and a number of European countries. It cannot be explained by changes in any of the major dietary components of the so-called 'Western diet'. Figure 2 shows the changes in the diet which have occurred in Britain from 1880 to 1970.[2] Looking at the two components of fibre, vegetable fibre and cereal fibre, there was a drift downwards in consumption of cereal fibre with an enormous temporary increase during the war, and a drift upwards in vegetable fibre, also with an increase during the war.

Table 1 shows the result of a study in which 53 children, aged 13–15, who had had appendicitis, had their diet measured by a 7-day weigh/food intake.[3] The results were compared with those from 2 sets of controls, who were children of the same age drawn either from the same class, or from the entire population of that age in Southampton. Initially results appeared interesting because total fibre consumption (i.e. all vegetable plus all cereal fibre) is a little lower in the cases than in either control groups. However, the cases also had lower intakes of energy, of protein, fat, carbohydrate and water (Table 2).[3] They were eating less of everything. This could have been an anorectic response to a recent illness, but they were also shorter in stature, which of course could not have been altered by recent surgery. The conclusion is that children in this study who had had appendicitis were shorter and ate less of all nutrients.

Further evidence linking diet and appendicitis comes from a study of the distribution of the disease throughout Britain and Ireland.[4] The places with the highest incidences of appendicitis are Anglesey, the Isle of Man, the

11

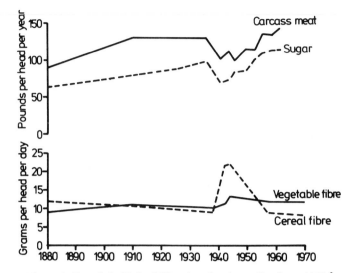

Figure 2. Trends in United Kingdom food supplies from 1880.[2]

TABLE 1. Mean intakes of dietary fibre (g/person/day) in appendicitis cases and age–sex matched controls

Source of fibre	Cases	Controls	Difference
All vegetables*	8.6	8.5	0.1 (−0.8,1.1)
Potatoes*	4.05	4.00	0.05 (−0.5,0.7)
Other than potatoes	4.65	4.68	−0.03 (−0.9,0.8)
Cereals	7.8	9.1	−1.3 (−2.6,0.1)
Bread*	2.8	3.1	−0.4 (−0.9,0.3)
Other cereal foods	4.5	5.1	−0.6 (−1.6,0.4)
Total	19.0	20.5	−1.5 (−3.0,0.0)

Figures in parentheses are 95% confidence intervals.
*log values in analysis of variance and in calculation of confidence intervals (geometric means shown in Table).[3]

Highlands of Scotland and the West of Ireland. A characteristic of the diet of these places is average or high intake of cereal fibre and one could infer that a high intake of cereal fibre is a cause of appendicitis. With vegetable intake the situation is different. Figure 3 shows a clear inverse relation between the intake of non-potato vegetables, that is mainly green vegetables, but also root vegetables, and the rates of appendicitis, adjusted for differences in age and sex.[5]

12

TABLE 2. Mean daily intakes of energy, nutrients, and water in appendicitis cases and age–sex matched controls

	Cases	Controls	Difference
Energy (MJ)	8.9	9.5	−0.6 (−1.2,0.03)
Protein (g)	65	68	−2.9 (−7.5,1.7)
Fat (g)	89	96	−6.6 (−14.4,1.2)
Carbohydrate (g)	281	298	−17 (−36.2)
Water* (g)	1287	1393	−108 (−209.1)

Figures in parentheses are 95% confidence intervals.
*log values in analysis of variance and in calculation of confidence intervals (geometric means shown in Table).[3]

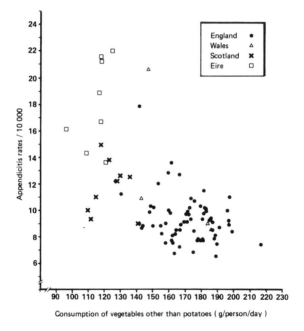

Figure 3. Consumption of vegetables other than potatoes and hospital discharge rates for acute appendicitis in 90 areas of Britain and Eire.[5]

It can be concluded that the only dietary component for which there is epidemiological evidence which is soundly based is non-potato vegetables. However, although implicated in some way, changes in non-potato vegetable

13

consumption could not explain the outstanding epidemiological characteristic of this disease. That is that when communities become industrialised/
westernised there are sharp rises in the incidence of appendicitis of the kind
seen in Britain at the beginning of the century. Subsequently appendicitis rates
decline, as in Europe and North America.

It is accepted that the ultimate event in appendicitis is the invasion of the
distal appendicular lumen by organisms which are habitually present within
the lumen.[6] Controversy centres on what are the earlier events which allow the
wall of the appendix to be breached by organisms which are habitually within
it. The suggestion that appendicitis usually results from occlusion of the neck
of the appendix by faecoliths is not consistent with the absence of faecoliths in
most removed appendices.[7] An alternative possibility is that an infection
might trigger off appendicitis by causing an immunological change, which
may be preceded or accompanied by swelling of the lymphatic tissue of the
neck of the appendix. The swelling may or may not lead to obstruction of the
distal appendix.[2] The infection model of particular interest in appendicitis is
that based on poliomyelitis.

The polio virus encountered in early infancy is known not to be pathogenic.
It does not damage neuronal tissue. The disease paralytic poliomyelitis is a
consequence of a first encounter with the virus at some time after early infancy.
It was noted fifty years ago that whereas westernisation leads to a fall in most
infective diseases, it leads to a rise in poliomyelitis. We are suggesting that
appendicitis is a disease of western hygiene and that delay in encounters with
enteric organisms, that is, delay from the critical period of infancy, renders the
appendix more susceptible to developing appendicitis when triggering infections are encountered in childhood and adolescence. In support of this are
several pieces of evidence. The first comes from the island of Anglesey, which
for various reasons did not acquire Western hygiene until after the Second
World War.[8] The censuses in 1951, 1961 and 1971 show the progressive
increase in the numbers of households in Anglesey which acquired fixed baths
and domestic hot water systems. Running hot water, which leads to fixed
baths and sinks, is a key element in Western hygiene and contributes to the
great decrease of childhood deaths from diarrhoeal disease that accompanies
westernisation. Within the framework of the 'hygiene' hypothesis Anglesey
would be predicted to have had an appendicitis epidemic later than other parts
of Britian, and this indeed was the case. The theatre records of Anglesey can be
used to calculate appendicitis rates in Anglesey from 1930 onwards. These
show a rise to high rates now at a time of continuing decline in the rates for
England, Wales and Scotland.

Secondly, we will consider the so-called 1946 cohort, a sample representing
all people born in England, Wales and Scotland during one week in 1946, who
have been followed up by the Medical Research Council ever since.[9] Those
who in early childhood did not have a bathroom in the house, that is, did not
have full Western hygiene, have had a lower rate of appendicitis (Table 3).[9]

Finally, there was a further study in Anglesey of 1860 people, of which 260
had had their appendices removed. People were simply classified into whether

TABLE 3. Appendicectomy and household amenities in 1946 cohort[9]

Amenity	Appendicectomy*	Relative risk	95% Confidence interval
Bathroom	136	1.0	
No bathroom	59	0.7	0.5 to 0.9
Hot water system	116	1.0	
No hot water system	81	0.9	0.7 to 1.2
Kitchen, exclusive use	170	1.0	
Kitchen, shared	23	0.9	0.6 to 1.4
All amenities	99	1.0	
Without one amenity	37	0.9	0.6 to 1.4
Without two amenities	50	0.8	0.5 to 1.1
Without three amenities	5	0.5	0.2 to 1.2

*Totals vary slightly because information not available in a few cases.

there was a bathroom in their house at birth and whether there was a bathroom in their house in later childhood. People who had a bathroom in the house at birth, that is, had Western hygiene, but then lived in houses without bathrooms, had double the risk of appendicitis.

On the packet of a certain famous breakfast cereal the question asked is: 'Are you missing a third of the fibre that you need every day?' For appendicitis the answer is, 'No, you are not'. The manufacturers will have to rationalise their sales of expensive cereal fragments in some other way. Appendicitis is a serious and often fatal disease. The incidence is rising in many parts of the world. Ideas about dietary fibre have been around for a long time, but my thesis is that it is time to abandon these outworn, outmoded ideas in the interests of a genuine search for the causes of this disease. At the moment the evidence suggests that the disease is not primarily related to the Western diet, but to the changes in Western housing.

In Northern Thailand the wealth flowing into rural communities in the aftermath of the Vietnamese war has led to a rebuilding of peasant housing and the adoption of Western hygiene. There has been a steep increase in appendicitis,[10] although no change in diet. It remains that of the traditional Chinese. In Soweto in Southern Africa near Johannesburg there has been a decline in fibre consumption, which is now around 6 grams per day. That is very low. Appendicitis, however, is uncommon. This is consistent with a community who have adopted the Western diet, but have not adopted the Western hygiene. There are many circumstances around the world where communities are changing. These provide considerable opportunity for exploring the causes of appendicitis.

15

REFERENCES

1 Rendle Short A. The causation of appendicitis. *Br J Surg* 1920;**8**:171–88.
2 Barker D J P. Acute appendicitis and dietary fibre: an alternative hypothesis. *Br Med J* 1985;**290**:1125–7.
3 Nelson M, Morris J, Barker D J P, Simmonds S. A case control study of acute appendicitis and diet in children. *J Epidemiol Community Health* 1986;**40**: 316–18.
4 Barker D J P, Morris J, Nelson M. Vegetable consumption and acute appendicitis in 59 areas in England and Wales. *Br Med J* 1986;**292**:927–30.
5 Barker D J P, Morris J. Acute appendicitis, bathrooms, and diet in Britain and Ireland. *Br Med J* 1988;**296**:953–5.
6 Aschoff L. (Translated by Pether G C) Appendicitis, its aetiology and pathology. London: Constable, 1932.
7 Trowell H C, Burkitt D P. Western diseases: their emergence and prevention. London: Edward Arnold, 1981.
8 Barker D J P, Morris J A, Simmonds S, Oliver R H P. Appendicitis epidemic following introduction of piped water to Anglesey. *J Epidemiol Community Health* 1988;**42**:144–8.
9 Barker D J P, Osmond C, Golding J, Wadsworth M E J. Acute appendicitis and bathrooms in three samples of British children. *Br Med J* 1988;**296**:956–8.
10 Chatbenchai W, Hedley A J, Ebrahim S B J, Aveemit S, Hoskyns E W, Dombal F T de. Acute abdominal pain and appendicitis in north east Thailand. *Paediatr Peri Epidemiol* 1989;**3**:448–59.
11 Barker D J P, Liggins A. Acute appendicitis in nine British towns. *Br Med J* 1981; **283**:1083–5.
12 Attwood S E A, Cafferkey M T, West A B. High appendicectomy rates in Ireland: why? *J Epidemiol Community Health* 1987;**41**:72–3.

ACKNOWLEDGEMENT

Figures and Tables reproduced by kind permission of British Medical Journal.

DISCUSSION

Prof Read   Your theory explained very nicely why the peaks of appendicitis develop, but why are we actually seeing a steady decline at the moment in industrialised countries.

Prof Barker   The hypothesis suggests that in the first stage of westernisation there is a reduction in infant experience of infection, but a continuing risk of encountering infections which would trigger appendicitis later on. The second phase, which we are in now, is where the continued improvement in hygiene has so reduced the level of infection in the community that although the population is vulnerable because of the absence of infant experience, it does not encounter the triggering infection. A recent study of army personnel posted abroad shows that those posted to Hong Kong or the Gulf have higher rates of appendicitis than those posted to Germany.

Dr Eastwood Can you tell me what you mean by appendicitis, because it has been shown that half of the appendices removed in this country are not inflamed. Creed has shown that a significant proportion of appendicectomies are for people with stress. Are your figures of appendicitis demonstrated by pathology rather than by appendicectomy?

Prof Barker The rate of removal of histologically normal appendices is around 25%. We have studied this in 9 towns in England and Wales and we have done a study in Anglesey.[8,11] There has also been a large study in Ireland.[12] The resulting figure is rather constant and so one can say with some assurance that variations of appendicectomy rates do not reflect differences in surgical practice. Indeed if they did, it would be remarkable to have produced such a high correlation with vegetable intake from place to place, because you would have to assume that surgeon's whimsicality was somehow related to their intake of green vegetables.

Dr Lean I have 3 questions. I had always assumed that the declining rates in appendicitis were associated with antibiotics or the confidence of physicians that children did not need surgery imminently. Secondly, you put a lot of store on food intake data. How confident are you that that actually reflects the food intake of children, and do episodic changes in food intake underly an episode of appendicitis? Finally, you might get some information on food intake if you looked at the size of the caecum or the thickness of the mucosa in those appendices removed which were inflamed compared with those which were not.

Prof Barker There have been a number of careful studies of changing rate of appendicitis in one hospital over time. These looked at whether the number of removed appendices have become more and more pathologically abnormal with sharpening of the diagnostic procedure. It is quite clear that this is not an explanation. As regards the general effect of antibiotics, it is a matter of speculation and I do not know. As regards the problems of measuring dietary intake, of course it is difficult to get children to record their diet of 7 days and get their parents to measure everything; and the argument that dietary things are going on but we cannot measure them runs well. However, I think that if dietary fibre was responsible for the immense epidemic of appendicitis which has occurred in Britain in the past 100 years, you would certainly expect to be able to identify differences between patients and controls with considerable ease.

FIBRE—ABSORPTION AND METABOLISM

Dr M A Eastwood
Consultant Physician
Western General Hospital
Edinburgh

Descriptions of the effects of dietary fibre on absorption and metabolism have repeatedly challenged conventional thought in gastroenterology and nutrition. When studies in fibre started there was a complacency in gastroenterology, with a belief that the contents of the gut were clear, buffered solutions containing a substance which was either absorbed passively or actively at a constant rate. From this one could extrapolate to the absorption of fat from an ingested meal in the intestine. Clearly however this was not the case, and the merit of fibre studies has been the study of what actually happens to a meal and how its residue is converted into faeces. The dietary bolus is a complex mixture which constantly changes in its chemical and physical properties along the gastrointestinal tract.

DEFINITION AND MEASUREMENT OF DIETARY FIBRE

Perhaps one of the most important contributions of fibre studies to human nutrition has been to re-examine the physical chemistry of events along the gastrointestinal tract.

An early and persistent problem was created by Hugh Trowell, one of the most important progenitors of the dietary fibre story. In the 1960s he insisted that a definition of dietary fibre was needed, and this definition resulted in problems. Dietary fibre was defined as the plant cell wall polysaccharides and lignin which were resistant to the enzymatic enzymes secreted in the human upper intestine. It is now appreciated that there are other nutrients which can also approximate to this definition. For example, resistant starch, and possibly protein and fat. The evolving concept of 'complex carbohydrates' to replace the term 'dietary fibre' or basing the definition of fibre on plant cell wall material may prove to be more useful.

Dietary fibre has effects on the gastrointestinal tract by

(1) modifying gastric emptying
(2) modifying intestinal absorption
(3) modulating sterol metabolism
(4) affecting fermentation in the caecum with the generation of hydrogen, carbon dioxide, methane and short chain fatty acids
(5) influencing stool weight.

The problem has been how is it possible to anticipate the biological activity of any particular dietary fibre in these areas. It is clear that the weight of grams of the fibre does not give any hint as to its biological potency. A gram of guar, a gram of bran, and a gram of pectin all have quite different spectra of activity. In addition to the limited value of the gravimetric values of dietary fibre we must consider physical characteristics and other biological properties, such as water holding capacity, cation exchange, bile acid adsorbent capacity, the ability to form a matrix for bacteria in the caecum and fermentation properties.

The most important property of dietary fibre is its association with water. Fibre will immobilise water in various phases.

(1) Water which is an inherent part of the structure of the fibre and is important in the format and chemistry of the fibre.

Freeze drying such fibre and removing the water results in irreversible changes.

(2) Water which is held in the matrix.

Such water suffuses through the fibre, and within that water nutrients and other solutes can be held.

(3) The third phase is free water and such water is readily removable.

Fibre can be regarded as a sponge passing along the gastrointestinal tract which absorbs this water.

GASTRIC EMPTYING AND SMALL BOWEL ABSORPTION

Fibre can have a modulating and slowing effect on gastric emptying and hence an effect on the rate at which nutrients associated with fibre will empty from the stomach and move into the duodenum. This is an important function of fibre. It is possible, however, to achieve the same slowing of absorption by eating more slowly.

Fibres of a viscous nature, of which guar is the most studied, slow absorption from the small intestine. However, that viscosity may change once the polymer passes into the varying osmolalities and pH's along the gastro-intestinal tract. These fibres do nonetheless slow the mixing and diffusion of solutes from the immobilised water into the free water, and hence absorption.

Fibres, gums and mucillages may also have an effect on pancreatic enzymes. In addition to this, fibre may influence the unstirred layer of the intestinal mucosa. The overall effect of such fibres is a resistance to nutrient convection currents so that solutes, i.e. the nutrients, are prevented from being absorbed. Such a delay means that the metabolic response of the body is much less abrupt than if the nutrient is taken as a solution.

The physical properties of fibre are all important. The analogy of the sponge is useful. The smaller the particle size of the sponge the less biologically potent it is. Biological potency is also affected by the way in which fibre is processed. Therefore a fibre source has to be defined by origin, physical characteristics and the method of preparation. Cellular structure is also important, so that the rate of absorption of glucose varies, depending on whether it is eaten in apple, pulp, or as apple juice.

The physical and chemical structure of starch may affect the absorption of glucose released after enzymatic hydrolysis. Amylase inhibitors which may accompany the fibre in the diet will affect hydrolysis of the starch. The processing of food, fibre and starch, may also affect absorption in the jejunum.

Therefore, a nutrient ingested with fibre will be absorbed over a lengthened period of time, and as a result of the expansion of the time taken for absorption there is a less profound metabolic response. Consequently the body has to make much less hormonal accommodation to that absorbed nutrient. This observation is becoming important in the treatment of maturity onset diabetics. A number of studies have looked at the time that it takes for the first part of a food bolus to pass from the mouth to the caecum. This is usually measured by examining the influence of various polysaccharides on the time taken for lactulose to produce hydrogen in the breath. The mouth to caecum transit time for lactulose solution on its own is between 90 and 120 minutes. This transit time is slowed with guar, tragacanth and, to a modest extent, pectin. Bran accelerates the time taken to the caecum.

FIBRE AND THE ENTEROHEPATIC CIRCULATION

Fibre has an effect on the enterohepatic circulation, particularly in relation to bile acids. Bile acids are held in the enterohepatic circulation and this influences sterol metabolism and the concentration of cholesterol in the blood, liver and bile. This latter has consequences for gallstone formation. One of the physical properties which has excited interest is the adsorption of bile acids to fibre, somewhat like cholestyramine. If bile acids are bound to fibre in the small intestine then the fibre:bile acid complex is drawn through the ileum into the caecum with the potential for an enhanced loss of bile acids from the enterohepatic circulation. This means that the enterohepatic circulation would be partially broken and the rate at which cholesterol is broken down to bile acids would be increased and the serum cholesterol decreased. However, those fibres which bind bile acids, such as wheat bran, have little or no effect on the serum cholesterol, gum arabic and pectin in the form of carrot. On the other hand, gum arabic reduces the serum cholesterol by 12 to 15%. Pectin, but not gum arabic, increases faecal bile acid excretion. Yet these fibres are totally fermented in the colon, as demonstrated by an increase in breath hydrogen. Other fibres such as potato fibre and karaya have no effect on the serum cholesterol or faecal bile acids, indicating the heterogeneity of biological effects of different fibres. Therefore it is necessary to rethink why bile acids or the enterohepatic circulation of bile acids are altered in association with polysaccharides. The action may be through the fermentation of fibre and the release of short chain fatty acids, or an effect of pH in the colon or adsorption to fibre in the ileum and the passage of more bile acids into the caecum.

FIBRE AND THE COLON

The colon consists of at least two organs. The right side of the colon functions as a fermenter, with a large bacterial mass numbering more than those of most organs in the body. On the left side in the descending and sigmoid colon bile is involved in the control of faecal gas, solid, liquid, and hence continence. In addition to this the colon absorbs sodium and water, and potassium is released into the colonic lumen.

The fermenter role can also be seen as having two aspects.

(1) There is nutrient salvage. The colon is the last port of call where absorption of nutrient takes place. Unabsorbed nutrients such as resistant starch, protein, fat, water and sodium may be absorbed in the proximal colon. Secreted muco-proteins are fermented and absorbed, and their end products absorbed as a nutrient source.

(2) The caecum also plays a part in the excretion system of bile secreted compounds, e.g. conjugated fat soluble materials with a molecular weight of ≥ 300 which were excreted in the bile; endogenous compounds, e.g. bile acid, bilirubin, hormones and exogenous materials, e.g. drugs and chemicals. The half life of many drugs is dictated by their fate in the colon. It may well be that such a half life is decided in part by the presence of fibre and the effect on enzyme induction.

There is therefore a complex system in the colon which is based on salvage and secretion. It is not known how the different facets of nutrients, bile and lumenal secretions interact. It is not known how the presence of fibre and other materials influence the induction of enzyme systems which will metabolise those other compounds passing into the caecum. It is possible that the whole system is dependent upon the size and enzyme activity of the bacterial mass. Knowledge of this relationship is very limited and yet the complexity is con-siderable. The fermentation system will be further complicated by the effect of osmolality, pH, electrolytes and the small molecular weight material. pH, redox potential and time of residence in the caecum will all influence fermen-tation patterns. Some materials will hasten the movement of fibre and other materials through the caecum (possibly bile acids) and others will slow the caecal residence time (e.g. short chain fatty acids). Studies of events in the caecum are somewhat derivative. It is necessary to look at caecal events in a somewhat second hand manner. For example, expired end products of fer-mentation. One simple method is to measure breath hydrogen production. Hydrogen is produced in the breath by almost every person. The concen-tration of this exhaled hydrogen decreases through the morning until lunch time and then increases in the postprandial period. This indicates that food and nutrition has an important role in hydrogen production. Hydrogen is significantly derived from the fermentation of dietary polysaccharides where mucoproteins may also be important. If an individual eats a polysaccharide or gum on a single occasion, e.g. gum arabic or pectin then there is no increment in breath hydrogen production. However, if the individual takes the gum for three weeks at 16 g per day, there is a subsequent increase in breath hydrogen production, which indicates an adaptation to the metabolism of that gum and consequently the evolution of hydrogen. This implies an adaptation of bacterial enzymes.

Methane production is constant and is individual to each person. In different populations there is a proportion of non-methane producers. In studies in Edinburgh we have shown that the percentage of methane producers in the population living on one side of a stretch of dual carriage-way was 80% while on the other side of the road it was 30%. There is no simple explanation for this. All individuals, to some extent, produce methane in the colon. The mass of methane producing bacteria appears to vary between individuals, and so it is that in some individuals a sufficiency of methane is produced to allow a spill over into the breath. It is quantitative production that dictates breath methane status but this does not explain why individuals produce large or small amounts of methane.

An important aspect of nutrition and physiology of the colon is the production of short chain fatty acid, acetate, propionate, and butyrate. The amount of short chain fatty acids produced in the rat caecum can be increased by giving fermentable gums, e.g. gum arabic and pectin. The amount of fatty acids produced is linearly related to the amount of gum or pectin ingested. However, if the amount of gum arabic is increased then there is a qualitative change in the short chain fatty acids, in that the butyrate decreases and the acetate increases. Butyrate is believed to be an obligate nutrient for the mucosa of the colon. Acetate is not metabolised by the colonic mucosa but is absorbed and thereafter it becomes a nutrient in the body at large. The other important short chain fatty acid is propionate which may influence cholesterol metabolism.

It has been suggested that gums and fibres make no calorific contribution to nutrition. Gum arabic and pectin are substantially fermented in an *in vitro* system with the evolution of short chain fatty acids and the metabolic value of these is of the order of 3 kCals per gram. Wheat bran results in very little production of short chain fatty acid. On the other hand eating gum arabic increases faecal fat excretion so that there is some loss of nutrient in this way.

STOOL WEIGHT

Stool weight and dietary fibre are closely related, but the relationship is very complex. Part of the problem is—what is normal stool weight? Stool collected from a range of normal individuals, not constipated, nor suffering from the irritable bowel syndrome, varied between 15 and 300 grams per day. For any individual in any week there is an enormous individual variation. It is difficult to derive a systematic result for stool weight from such wide data. There is a linear relationship between the amount of fibre in the diet and the weight of stool mass. The values which range between 15 and 280 grams are on a fibre intake of between 7 and 30 grams per day. Such a fibre intake is substantially less than that which has been reported for Cambridge.

Stool consists of 75% water. Of the dry material half is bacteria, half is fibre. Wheat bran passes through the gastrointestinal tract like a sponge, minimally fermented by bacteria, and the extent to which bran increases stool weight depends on the water holding capacity of the wheat bran. Therefore the greater the water holding capacity, i.e. the less cooked and milled, the greater

23

the effect on stool weight. Fruit and vegetables are fermented by bacteria. The bacterial mass may increase, also resulting in an increase in stool weight. These are quite different actions. Wheat bran increases stool weight in a predictable way, dependent on the water holding capacity; the effects of fruit and vegetables are variable, but increase stool weight by increasing bacterial mass. There is a linear relationship or dose response curve for wheat bran and stool weight; the more eaten the greater the stool weight. There is an inverse relationship between the amount of wheat bran and the transit time. It does not matter what the original stool weight was, there is always a *pro rata* increment with wheat bran. The type of bran does not matter. In a study comparing Canadian Red Spring wheat used in bread making and French soft wheat used in cake making, the important effect of the bran was the coarseness of the bran flake rather than the origin. Fine bran has little effect on stool weight at 20 grams per day, whereas coarse bran has a substantial effect.

Different fibres do different things. The biological properties of dietary fibre in the gut are

(1) modulation of absorption in the fore gut
(2) modification of sterol metabolism
(3) inducement of caecal fermentation
(4) increase of stool weight by water holding capacity or by bacteria.

Each fibre will have different biological effects in each of these areas.

FURTHER READING

Trowell H, Burkitt D, Heaton K. (eds). Dietary Fibre; fibre depleted foods and disease. Academic Press, London, 1985.
Vahouny G V, Kritchevsky D. Dietary Fiber. Plenum Press, New York, 1986.

DISCUSSION

Prof Bloom   You stated that bran fibre does not affect bile salt absorption. Cholestyramine and other resin agent studies have clearly shown a relationship between binding of bile salts; the better the resin binds bile salts and the more resin used, the greater the lowering of cholesterol, so if bile salts are bound by bran, perhaps bran puts cholesterol up. Or does bran not bind bile salts as well as cholestyramine and therefore it is all a rather minor effect?

Dr Eastwood   Yes, I think that wheat bran has about a tenth or a fifth of the adsorbent properties of cholestyramine. Even cholestyramine, which would be predicted to decrease the cholesterol by 30%, in fact only reduces serum cholesterol by 6–10%, and so is disappointing in this respect. There are two important points in reply to your question. Firstly, binding in the gut may not be the most important mechanism in influencing sterol metabolism. Eriksen's experiments described in the 1950s showed that cannulating the common bile duct resulted in an acceleration of bile acid excretion and cholesterol catabolism. Secondly, if binding of bile acids is important, it may be that bran is not a sufficiently good binder to influence cholesterol metabolism, since all the studies, with one exception, have shown no effect of bran on cholesterol.

Prof Read   Could I ask you to speculate on two points? Firstly, to what extent can we usefully salvage any protein that might be malabsorbed in the intestine for use by the body? Secondly, I have many awfully constipated patients with an enormous bacterial cell mass and a prolonged transit time who complain of headaches, sickness, tiredness and a multitude of other complaints. Do you think they are being poisoned by colonic metabolites that have escaped detoxification by the liver? Is colonic fermentation much more important clinically than we have realised hitherto?

Dr Eastwood   The answer to the first question is that I do not know about the protein. Perhaps it provides an important nitrogen source to bacteria and hence has effects which may be indirect in terms of bacterial enzyme systems, rather than the colon being an important site of nitrogen conservation. It would be unfortunate if there was a resurrection of the Metchnikoff colonic stasis and ill-health philosophy. He believed that the reason that Russian Georgians lived longer was because they ate yoghurt. One of the reasons why Georgians appeared to live longer was a result of ploys to avoid military service wherein sons took their father's birth certificate to avoid conscription. So it was more complicated than just yoghurt.

The bowel is important in the enterohepatic circulation, in the conservation of biliary excreted hormones and other chemicals. This is important in conserving all manner of biologically active substances, some of which may affect man.

THE CHOLESTEROL CONNECTION

Linda M Morgan
Senior Research Fellow
University of Surrey
Guildford

A high plasma cholesterol level is one of the risk factors strongly associated with atherosclerosis-related diseases, particularly ischaemic heart disease (IHD).[1] In the early 1980s, dietary recommendations were drawn up, particularly regarding fat intake.[2] Their purpose was to lower the risk of coronary heart disease by reducing the plasma total cholesterol level (or, more specifically, low density lipoprotein (LDL) cholesterol) whilst maintaining high density lipoprotein (HDL) cholesterol, believed to be protective against CHD. The observation that the prevalence of CHD appears low in populations consuming high fibre diets[3] has motivated research into the possible hypocholesterolaemic effects of dietary fibre.

Diets enriched with non-soluble fibre (cellulose and some hemicelluloses e.g. as in wheat bran) do not consistently affect circulating cholesterol levels, although wheat bran has been shown to decrease liver cholesterol storage in animal studies.[4] In contrast, water-soluble fibres (pectins, gums, mucillages and some hemi-celluloses) can exert significant hypocholesterolaemic effects, with most of the decrease in cholesterol being seen in the LDL fraction, the HDL fraction being variously reported as unchanged, or occasionally lowered.

The short-term effects of dietary fibre supplementation on circulating lipid levels in normocholesterolaemic human subjects were demonstrated in the following study.[5] The effect of a 20 g/day dietary supplementation of either guar gum (galactomannan, 100% soluble fibre), sugar beet fibre ($\sim 25\%$ pectic substances, 35% hemi-celluloses) and wheat bran is shown in Figure 1. Total cholesterol levels were reduced by 12% and 5% respectively during guar and sugar beet fibre supplementation, but were unchanged by wheat bran supplementation. HDL-cholesterol, triglycerides, glucose and insulin levels remained unchanged throughout the study. Subjects' dietary fat intake also remained constant throughout this study at a level of 38% total energy intake—typical of current UK diets and somewhat higher than the current dietary recommendations. Conflicting results from earlier studies may have arisen because insufficient attention had been paid to the compositional variation of the diet, particularly with respect to fat. There is some evidence that the level of fat intake may modify the influence of various fibres on lipid metabolism. Animal studies have shown, for example, that pectin is less effective against a background of high fat intake.[6]

The fall in cholesterol levels obtained, at least with guar supplementation, appears to be dose-related. One of the problems associated with the use of

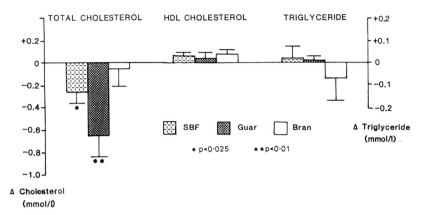

Figure 1. Effects of 20 g/d fibre supplementation for 14 d on fasting plasma lipids in 12 healthy normolipidaemic subjects.

soluble fibres such as pectin and guar is their lack of palatability, with consequent difficulty in incorporating enough fibre into the diet to exert a significant hypocholesterolaemic effect. Oat products, such as rolled oats, contain large amounts of water-soluble fibre and are one of the more palatable alternatives. Falls in total cholesterol levels ranging from 13–23% have been reported following 100 g/day oat bran supplementation in hyperlipidaemic patients,[7] but oat products appear less effective at lowering cholesterol in normal subjects.[8] Legumes are also effective hypocholesterolaemic agents. Whilst the majority of legume seeds do not feature widely in the British diet, the popularity of baked beans (*Phaseolus vulgaris*) in tomato sauce is exceptional. Their wide acceptability is unique amongst high-fibre products, increasing their potential for prophylactic and therapeutic use.

A recent study[9] on the effect of daily consumption of a 450 g tin of baked beans in normocholesterolaemic men has shown a 12% reduction in total cholesterol levels after 14 days. In this study, subjects' fat intake fell by 15% during the period of dietary intervention. The observed changes in plasma cholesterol could not, however, be explained in terms of dietary fat displacement as a period of dietary supplementation with spaghetti, producing a similar degree of fat displacement, was without effect on cholesterol.

There are several mechanisms by which plant fibres can exert their hypocholesterolaemic effect. The best investigated hypothesis to explain the action of the soluble fibres is that of altered bile acid metabolism. Soluble fibre-rich diets usually increase faecal bile acid excretion.[10] Bile acid malabsorption stimulates bile acid synthesis from cholesterol, and the body pool of cholesterol is decreased via up-regulation of hepatic apoprotein B receptors.[11] However, oat bran and beans which are rich in soluble fibre have been reported to lower serum cholesterol in hypercholesterolaemic subjects without

27

significantly increasing bile acid excretion. Short-chain fatty acids, formed from the colonic fermentation of fibre polysaccharides, are almost completely absorbed into the portal vein.[12] They have been shown to inhibit hepatic cholesterol synthesis in animal studies and provide a possible alternative explanation for the hypocholesterolaemic effect of oat and bean fibre. Constituents other than fibre in legumes may also contribute significantly to their hypocholesterolaemic effect. Plant sterols, found in leguminous seeds, have very similar structures to cholesterol but are poorly absorbed from the intestine. Pharmacological doses of such sterols lower plasma cholesterol levels by inhibiting the absorption of cholesterol from the intestine[13] but no information is available on the magnitude of contribution made by plant sterols to the cholesterol lowering effect of legumes. Saponins, found in relatively large quantities in many legume varieties, including *Phaseolus vulgaris*, have potent hypocholesterolaemic effects and it has been suggested that their presence in legumes is a major determinant of the hypocholesterolaemic effect.[14] Saponins are not normally absorbed from the gut; thus their activity must take place within the GI tract. Saponins may either induce the binding of bile acids to dietary fibre, or combine with cholesterol and bile acids in the intestine to form micelles, the contents of which are not available for absorption—phenomena which have both been demonstrated *in vitro*.

The motivation for much of the work on the cholesterol lowering properties of fibre has been based on the importance of cholesterol as a biochemical marker identifying individuals at increased risk for CHD. Recent evidence has, however, indicated that serum apolipoproteins may be better discriminators in assessing CHD risk than are conventional cholesterol or lipoprotein-cholesterol measurements.[15] Apolipoproteins are genetically determined

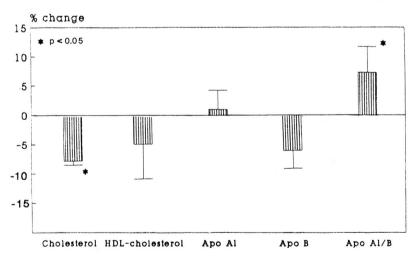

Figure 2. Effects of 20 g/d sugar beet fibre supplementation on serum cholesterol and apolipoprotein levels in 6 non-insulin dependent diabetics.

28

components of lipoproteins, or lipid transport particles, and influence the conformation, receptor binding and metabolism of the lipoproteins. In particular, high values of apolipoprotein B together with low values of apolipoprotein A1 are associated with a high predictive risk of CHD. Apolipoprotein levels are modified by changes in dietary fat intake which affect cholesterol levels.[16] The effect of fibre-rich diets on serum apolipoprotein levels is largely unknown. We have recently demonstrated, in a small series of diabetic subjects, a highly significant correlation between changes in Apo B and total cholesterol levels when supplementing their diet with 20 g sugar beet fibre daily. Apo A1 and HDL cholesterol levels were unchanged but the Apo A1/B ratio was significantly raised during the period of fibre supplementation (Fig. 2). This suggests that the fibre supplementation not only caused loss of cholesterol from LDL, but also reduced the concentration of circulating LDL particles.

Further study, extending biochemical investigations on the effect of dietary fibre supplementation to apolipoprotein concentrations and other parameters of lipid metabolism, will provide more information on mechanisms of action and a better assessment of the benefits of fibre consumption in lowering the risk of CHD.

REFERENCES

1 Shaper A G, Pocock S J. Risk factors for ischaemic heart disease in Britain. *Br Heart J* 1987;**57**:11–16.
2 Committee on Medical Aspects of Food Policy. Diet and cardiovascular disease. *Report on Health and Social Subjects* **28**; London: HMSO: 1984.
3 Anderson J W. Health implications of wheat fibre. *J Clin Nutr* 1985;**41**:1103–12.
4 Chen W J L, Anderson J W. Effects of guar gum and wheat bran on lipid metabolism of rats. *J Nutr* 1979;**109**:1028–34.
5 Morgan L M, Tredger J A, Williams C A, Marks V. Effects of sugar beet fibre on glucose tolerance and circulating cholesterol levels. *Proc Nutr Soc* 1988;**47**: 185A.
6 Vigne J L, Lairon D, Borel P *et al.* Effect of pectin, wheat bran, and cellulose on serum lipids and lipoproteins in rats fed on a low or high-fat diet. *Br J Nutr* 1987; **58**:405–13.
7 Anderson J W, Gustafson N J. Hypocholesterolaemic effects of oat and bean products. *Am J Clin Nutr* 1988;**48**:749–53.
8 Judd P A, Truswell A S. The effect of rolled oats on blood lipids and faecal steroid excretion in man. *Am J Clin Nutr* 1981;**34**:2061–7.
9 Shutler S M, Bircher G M, Tredger J A, Morgan L M, Walker A F, Low A G. The effect of daily baked bean (*Phaseolus vulgaris*) consumption on the plasma lipid levels of young normocholesterolaemic men. *Br J Nutr* 1989;**61**:257–65.
10 Kay R M, Truswell A S. Effect of citrus pectin on blood lipids and faecal steroid excretion in man. *Am J Clin Nutr* 1977;**30**:171–5.
11 Brown M S, Goldstein J L. A receptor-mediated pathway for cholesterol homeostasis. *Science* 1986;**232**:34–47.
12 Cummings J H. Short-chain fatty acids in the human colon. *Gut* 1981;**22**:763–79.
13 Lees A M, Mok H Y I, Lees R S *et al.* Plant sterols as cholesterol-lowering agents: clinical trials in patients with hypercholesterolaemia and studies of sterol balance. *Atherosclerosis* 1977;**28**:325–38.

14 Shutler S M, Walker A F, Low A G. The cholesterol-lowering effect of legumes II: effects of fibre, sterols, saponins and isoflavones. *Hum Nutr: Food Sci Nutr* 1987;**41F**:87–102.
15 Naito H K. New diagnostic tests for assessing coronary heart disease risk. *Recent aspects of diagnosis and treatment of lipoprotein disorders—impact on prevention of Atherosclerotic diseases,* pp. 49–62. Alan R Liss, Inc.: 1988.

DISCUSSION

Prof Bloom How would you compare the efficacy of a high soluble fibre diet for lowering cholesterol with a high polyunsaturated diet?

Dr Morgan We are currently setting up studies to look at the two in concert by stepwise putting people onto a fat modified diet, then looking at the additional possible benefits of adding fibre to that, but it is very difficult to disentangle the two. As we saw with the baked bean study, if you add fibre to any great extent as a food product, as opposed to a dietary supplement like guar, you inevitably displace fat from the diet and it makes interpretation of the results very difficult.

Prof Read Putting people on a bean diet is said to reduce insulin secretion. If someone eats a meal containing beans instead of other sources of carbohydrate, what effect would this have on cholesterol synthesis in the liver?

Dr Morgan A reduction in insulin secretion should have a net hypocholesterolaemic effect, which is a change in the right direction. I presume you are talking about post prandial insulin secretion.

Prof Marks It may be due to an effect upon the gut hormones, which are insulinotropic; or it could be a result of a lower rise in blood glucose, because the whole thing reduces the glycaemic index.
    Dave Jenkins showed in the nibbling versus gorging studies that if a set dietary intake was taken almost like a drip feed throughout the day, there was a reduction in total cholesterol at the same time as there was a reduction in insulin and C peptide production. Whether one was causal to the other is not known, but would be in accord of what we know about cholesterol synthesis.

Audience Regarding your spaghetti results and the lowering of the HDL, is there any resistant starch in spaghetti that might be fermented? Presumably your fibre is a chemically defined fibre?

Dr Morgan This was a standard tin of spaghetti, we did not measure the resistant starch content of it, but I think it is likely to be low.

Audience So that could not explain it, and neither could any change in fat?

Dr Morgan   It is possibly due to the accompanying changes in refined sugar consumption, which went up with both beans and spaghetti.

Audience   Do you know of any studies on normal blood cholesterol levels in people without a colon?

Dr Morgan   I am not aware of any studies that have been done. Perhaps we should throw that open to the audience.

Prof Marks   There are sufficient people walking round who have not got colons. They are or have been sick for one reason or another, and it would be an interesting thing to run through the laboratory results on them.

Dr Eastwood   The kinetics of bile acids in patients with an ileostomy are quite different from those in patients with an intact colon, so one would not be comparing like with like. It is so obvious but nobody has done it.

Prof Bloom   You would have to have colostomy patients rather than ileostomy patients for the reasons you have specified. Bile salt absorption in the terminal ileum would be affected.

Prof Marks   Yes, you get a dramatic change in the physiology of the ileum when you actually remove the colon, I believe.

Dr Eastwood   Serum concentration alters by an estimated 10–17% and the half life of bile acids changes quite significantly.

Prof Marks   Then one would have to look at the incidence of cardiovascular disease in people who had undergone colectomy for a non malignant disease. There are quite a lot of Stanley Aylett's patients still around in whom he removed the colon for ulcerative colitis and joined up the ileum to the rectum. If one could collect them all together it would be an interesting study.

Audience   Do you modify diet in order to prevent diarrhoea, which is quite a major problem, so that these patients eat very funny food?

Audience   They do not in fact modify their diet.

Mr Moran   There is a major increase in bacterial flora in the ileum after ileostomy, so you get a lot of fermentation in the terminal ileum, which becomes almost a new colon.

Prof Marks   What happens if you join up the ileum to the rectum?

Mr Moran   You get bacterial flora in the rectum and terminal ileum.

Prof Bloom   Dr Morgan, what happens to the gut hormones?

Dr Morgan   I am sure you are familiar with the effect of guar on some insulin stimulating gut hormones. We are looking at a few more of them, but to date, not a great deal happens.

Prof Marks   What about with sugar beet fibre?

Dr Morgan   Sugar beet fibre is quite interesting from the point of view of insulin stimulating gut hormones. Sugar beet fibre improves glucose tolerance, but has no effect on insulin secretion. Unlike guar, which lowers both GIP and insulin secretion post prandially, sugar beet actually increases GIP secretion, which may account for the differences in insulin secretion that we observe with the two fibres.

Prof Bloom   We know that impaired glucose tolerance increases ischaemic heart disease, and is a major cause of death and disability in those with even minor diabetes. If you have a better than normal glucose tolerance, do you have less than normal ischaemic heart disease, in the same way that the cholestyramine experiments have proved that when the cholesterol comes down ischaemic heart disease gets less. It is the only circumstance where it has been really proven, but improvement in carbohydrate tolerance may be as important as lowering cholesterol.

Dr Morgan   It is an attractive hypothesis, but difficult to prove. The problems that people have had substantiating the third tenet of the lipid hypothesis illustrate the difficulties involved in substantiating a similar claim for carbohydrate tolerance.

Prof Marks   Professor Bloom is alluding to the strong feeling that hyper-insulinaemia or hyperproinsulinaemia is a factor in the pathogenesis of atherosclerosis. If you reduce the amount of insulin or pro-insulin being secreted you might reduce atherosclerosis. Vigorous exercise may be beneficial, because it is known to have this sort of effect. However, nobody has compared healthy people who have better glucose tolerance with those who have normal glucose tolerance.

GENERAL DISCUSSION—AM

Prof Marks It is fashionable to take concoctions of micro-organisms or live yoghurt, available from so-called Health shops, to change the fermentation in your bowel. Is there any reason to believe that any of these micro-organisms chew up one form of dietary fibre more than another?

Dr Eastwood As I understand it, the colonic flora are remarkably stable, but the methods of classifying them are not good. Identification can be very dependent on the media in which particular organisms are grown. Therefore organisms will adapt to the medium which is used for identification, and results are determined in part by the methods rather than of the type of bacteria. With those limitations we know from various studies that it is very difficult to alter the spectrum of bacteria by fibre content of the diet. In contrast is the production of enzymes by that constant bacterial flora; where there can be modulation of enzyme activity in response to the nutrients that pass to the caecum.

Prof Bloom Many people with chronic acne are on tetracycline for years, which certainly modifies gut bacteria. In what way has probably not been studied. Also is there any difference between the female and the male colonic metabolism? There is certainly a difference in ischaemic heart disease, perhaps not too much in cholesterol, but oestrogens and progesterone, for example, affect the motor activity of the muscle of the large bowel. We know that constipation is much more common in females. If we give supplementation of non absorbable, but fermentable sugars, in particular our sponsor's product, lactulose, would it affect any parameters that we are looking at?

Prof Read In connection with bacterial flora, if you decimate the colonic flora with broad spectrum antibiotics, then you cause quite a lot of changes related to the overgrowth of organisms that are normally kept in check. In a convincing study recently the incidence of severe post operative sepsis was greater if broad spectrum antibiotics had been given to cleanse the colon. The use of live yoghurt, lactobacillus, to recolonise the colon was advocated and preliminary results were quite good. The situation is similar with colitis and pseudo-membraneous colitis. In people on broad spectrum antibiotics, a particular organism, *Clostridium difficile*, can gain ascendance and cause a very severe colitis. There may be some changes in ordinary ulcerative colitis with the same sort of pathogenesis. Some years ago a Swedish group were actually giving a faecal enema to people with pseudo-membraneous colitis. I do not think it will catch on, but nevertheless the results were very interesting.

Audience There was a recent paper in the Lancet where one of the authors had ulcerative colitis and he cleared out his flora with antibiotics, then replaced it with a healthy person's flora. The ulcerative colitis did not recur, or the symptoms were very much depressed. Concerning preparations from

Health Food shops, they are mostly lactobacilli, which as far as I know are not terribly good at fermenting fibre. The organisms usually studied for fibre fermentation are bacteroides. If you are taking large enough supplements of lactobacilli your count of lactobacilli in the colon does go up and the bacteroides count will decrease somewhat, so they certainly could affect fermentation. However, I do not think anybody has studied that. Other bacterial enzymes in the colon are altered if you give supplementations of lactobacilli, but as soon as supplementation stops they return to their previous level.

Prof Marks   I have been involved in work with xylitol, which in large doses gets into the colon, and actually changes the microflora of the human colon. It reverts when subjects stop taking xylitol, but whether that is a good or a bad thing we do not know.

Dr Whitehead, Duphar   We have been told this morning that fibre is good for you, but what should people be advised by health professionals to take in the form of a high fibre diet? Should this be adjusted depending on whether one wants to avoid colorectal cancer or cardiovascular disease, or should it be general?

Dr Eastwood   The answer to that is restricted because few dose response curves have ever been done on pure types or mixed fibre. Most of the attempts to establish a recommended daily allowance take one of the following 4 areas: gastric emptying, sterol metabolism, fermentation or stool weight in isolation. It is possible to identify one or two fibres in which a dose response curve has been studied and make a guess from that. It has been suggested that as far as laxation in the colon is concerned something approximately between 20 or 30 grams of cereal fibre would be recommended. The London food group have suggested—and this has now become part of fibre mythology—that 30 grams of fibre, half from cereal and half from fruit and vegetable sources, would be reasonable. However, as important as what one eats is what ones parents died from and also where one lives. For example, in a Scottish population, the rates of carcinoma of the colon and coronary artery disease are substantially greater than in the south of England. The Scottish diet does not contain an enhanced cereal content. Perhaps a reasonable recommendation at the moment would be 30 grams, half cereal and half fruit and vegetable, but there is absolutely no basis upon which to justify that.

Prof Marks   I cannot let the opportunity pass without mentioning the syndrome that I dubbed 'Bran Belly' where people who have been led to believe that fibre is good have consumed more of it than was appropriate for them and have fermented it in their colons to such an extent that they have distended bellies and feel very uncomfortable. The best treatment for them is to advise them not to eat such 'healthy' food. Those of us who are misguided enough to persist in eating uncooked muesli, if we are one of the group of people who ferment these things, know this from our own experience.

Therefore I do not believe that fibre is good for you, full stop. I subscribe to the idea that under certain circumstances it is a sensible thing to have a diet which is well balanced and contains perhaps 30 grams of fibre.

Prof Read   I want to ask Professor Barker about the concept that exposure to certain micro-organisms at an early stage in development is important in protecting against appendicitis. What does he perceive to be the mechanism there, is this a kind of immunological tolerance? In connection with that, what is the period of time over which exposure might be important? If the critical period of time is the time when babies are fed milk, is there any difference in subsequent appendicitis rates between breast fed and bottle fed babies? Finally, if you take the appendix out of somebody, are they then more susceptible to other conditions that might affect the colon against which the appendix might protect by maintaining the bacteria in the fermenting chamber?

Prof Barker   Obviously it is important to understand the mechanism by which the hygiene hypothesis operates. One thing that the fibre hypothesis has demonstrated is how relatively unhelpful epidemiology is without understanding of the process. We have understood in general terms that paralytic polio operates on the model I described, but we know little about the critical time. Presumably there is some clearly defined period in infancy when polio infection is protective. We understand very little about how this operates, and the same applies to appendicitis. This tremendous interest in the Western diet to the exclusion of other interests has meant that we know little about these things. I am not aware of studies which have related breast and bottle feeding to the incidence of appendicitis, but it is a very interesting suggestion. It could be, within limits, answered readily from the three cohorts of children born in 1946, 1958 and 1970, who are the three national cohorts for which we have data. Your third question about whether people who have had their appendix removed are thereby liable to other diseases, perhaps somebody in the audience knows the answer to this. My understanding is that the appendix is of extreme importance in early life in assisting in the establishment of gut immunity. Its function may decline thereafter, so perhaps one would not expect removal at the age of 50 to have consequences.

Prof Garrow   You drew attention to the similarity between the aetiology of appendicitis and polio. Do the peaks of these two coincide? Secondly, is there an animal model for appendicitis on which a series have been tested?

Prof Barker   No, the peaks do not coincide. The first polio epidemics were in Scandinavia at the end of the last century, but there was no information about the peaks of appendicitis in Scandinavia. The peak of the poliomyelitis epidemic in this country was just before and after the Second War, so it was about ten years later than the peak of the appendicitis epidemic should have been. The second question is very important. It has been suggested that we could study appendicitis in large primates, but the current financial restraints on medical research makes this rather difficult.

Audience   Could Professor Barker comment on epidemiology, as there seems to be a lack of correlation between constipation and diverticular disease. I am thinking of the Middle East, for example, Saudi Arabia, where they have a traditional diet which is very low in vegetable fibre, they do get a lot of constipation, but diverticular disease is virtually unknown.

Prof Barker   Yes, here again you have a situation like colon cancer where there is a broad international ecological relation between fibre consumption and certain diseases—diverticulosis and colon cancer—and this relationship is greatly helped if you ignore China. However, when you examine this relationship in more detail it starts to break down. Work which would show a relationship in individuals is obviously difficult to do. I agree there are methodological problems in establishing relations in individuals between fibre consumption and colon cancer. Clearly if it operates at all then it operates over long periods, so I think the evidence relating lack of dietary fibre to the onset and incidence of diverticulosis does not exist. The ideas about diverticulosis centre around the benefits of fibre in treating people with established disease, which is another matter. I cannot comment on your observations in the Middle East.

DIETARY FIBRE, FOOD INTAKE AND OBESITY

Professor J S Garrow
and Dr Allison Owens
Lecturer
Rank Department of Human Nutrition
St Bartholomew's Hospital Medical College
London

INTRODUCTION

A potential role for dietary fibre has been postulated in both the prevention and treatment of obesity.[1,2] Although epidemiological evidence suggests that a diet low in fibre may increase the tendency to obesity,[1] it is very difficult to separate the effect of fibre from that of other dietary variables and as yet little evidence exists to implicate a low fibre intake *per se*. This paper concentrates on the value of dietary fibre in the management of obesity and uses the term 'dietary fibre' as defined by Cummings[3] to mean the sum of lignin and undigested non-starch polysaccharides in foods.

The successful treatment of obesity requires the creation of a negative energy balance by either reducing the available energy from food and/or increasing energy expenditure. Claims made in the 'popular diet press' promise that a high fibre diet can help achieve this goal since it is 'more satisfying and filling', the implication being that it can help to reduce food and hence energy intake, and 'a larger proportion of calories consumed will be undigested'.[4] Evidence for these claims is reviewed.

DIETARY FIBRE AND ENERGY INTAKE

The ingestion of fibre by man may promote satiety, decrease the caloric density of food, increase the amount of effort required to chew food and alter the palatability of the diet.[5,1,6] If true, fibre might be expected to reduce the overall energy intake in man and thereby aid the treatment of obesity. Unfortunately, few studies convincingly demonstrate this (Table 1).

Grimes and Gordon[7] reported a lower intake of wholemeal bread compared with white bread when subjects were asked to 'eat bread to a point of comfortable fullness' and suggested that this provided evidence that a low fibre diet results in an increased energy intake. No quantitative data on bread consumption were given and no attempt was made to account for possible differences in palatability of the breads. In contrast, Bryson *et al.*[8] found no difference in the lunch-time or subsequent 24 hour energy intake of volunteers offered a lunch of either white or wholemeal bread with butter and jam. A more recent study of female volunteers showed no significant effect of a 'high fibre' breakfast on the total energy consumption at lunch.[9] These three studies all investigated

TABLE 1. Effect of dietary fibre on food and total energy intake in man

Authors	Fibre	Dose (g)	Administration	Subjects	Duration	Control	Food/Energy intake
Effect of high fibre meal:							
Grimes & Gordon[7]	Wheat bran	Unlimited	Wholemeal bread	Lean	1 meal	White bread	Reduced bread intake at test meal
Bryson et al.[8]	Wheat bran	Unlimited	Wholemeal bread	Lean	1 meal	White bread	No effect at test meal or over next 24 h
Porikos & Hagamen[10]	Methyl-cellulose	7	High fibre bread	Obese Lean	1 meal	Low fibre bread (<1 g DF)	Reduced food intake at test meal in obese only
Burley et al.[9]	Wheat bran + Guar gum	12	Branflakes + Guar bread	Lean	1 meal	Cornflakes + White bread (3 g DF)	No effect on energy intake at next meal
Effect of pre-meal supplements:							
Evans & Miller[11]	Guar gum or Methyl-cellulose	10 g/d	Granules	Obese Lean	1 week	Unsupplemented period	Both fibres reduced energy intake. Greatest effect in obese
Rigaud et al.[13]	Mixed veg. citrus + grain fibre	7 g/d	Tablets	Lean	4 weeks	Starch + Lactose tablets (<1 g DF/d)	No effect on energy intake over study
Stevens et al.[12]	Psyllium gum, Wheat bran or both	23 g/d	Crackers	Obese	2 weeks	Low fibre cracker (4 g DF/d)	Energy intake reduced by gum or gum + wheat bran only
Effect of high fibre foods:							
Kahaner et al.[14]	Wheat bran	11 g/d	All bran cereal	Lean	3 weeks	Unsupplemented period (4 g DF/d)	Energy intake increased

non-obese subjects over short time periods. The results cannot be extrapolated to obese volunteers since other workers have shown that consumption of a methylcellulose pre-load (6.6 g dietary fibre) reduced food intake at the following test meal in obese subjects only,[10] thus suggesting that obese and lean volunteers may respond differently to dietary fibre in the short-term.

Effects of dietary fibre on energy intake can only be of potential use in the management of obesity if long-term reductions in energy consumption occur. It is regrettable that data on the chronic effects of fibre consumption on energy intake in man are limited and appear inconclusive. When taken as a pre-meal supplement for 1 week, a daily intake of 10 g of fibre provided as methyl-cellulose or guar gum granules significantly reduced the mean daily energy intake of obese and lean subjects by 10% compared with unsupplemented periods.[11] In a later study Stevens et al.[12] showed 7% and 5% reductions in the energy intake of obese volunteers when they consumed 23 g of fibre per day as pre-meal supplements of psyllium gum or psyllium gum plus wheat bran crackers respectively. These data were not confirmed when a lower level of dietary fibre (7.3 g per day) provided as mixed vegetable, citrus and grain fibre tablets was fed to non-obese volunteers before each meal for 4 weeks.[13] Wheat bran failed to reduce energy intake when given either as pre-meal supplements providing 23 g of fibre per day[12] or as a high fibre breakfast cereal which increased the total daily fibre consumption to 104 g.[14] Duncan et al.[15] showed that both lean and obese subjects reduced their *ad libitum* daily energy consumption from 3000 to 1570 kcal when they switched from a high energy density, low fibre diet to a low energy density, high fibre diet but were unable to attribute this to a direct effect of fibre since the diets differed in other respects including fat and sugar content.

SATIETY

Promotion of intestinal satiety may be the way in which dietary fibre can help to achieve the decrease in energy intake necessary for weight loss.[4] Suggested mechanisms include an increased chewing time causing a promotion of saliva and gastric juice secretion, a greater gastric distention due to the water absorptive capacity of some fibres and a reduction in the post-prandial glycaemia and insulinaemia due to a decreased rate of carbohydrate digestion and absorption and a prolonged rate of gastric emptying.[6,16] Soluble fibre sources might be expected to have the greatest effect since it has been shown that guar gum delays gastric emptying time and that gastric emptying time is significantly correlated with a subjective measure of satiety in obese patients.[17] In addition, it is the soluble, non-cellulosic fibres that have the greatest reducing effect on post-prandial blood glucose, insulin and gastrointestinal hormone levels in man. For further details of mechanisms controlling hunger the reader is referred to the extensive review of Castonguay et al.[18]

There have been many attempts to determine the effects of fibre on hunger and satiety in man but interpretation of the results is made difficult due to differences in the type, dose and mode of administration of the fibre, in the study length and in the methodology used to assess satiety or hunger. For purposes of this review data have been divided into effects of dietary fibre on hunger ratings over periods of up to 24 hours (Table 2) and over 1–12 weeks (Table 3).

Despite differences in methodologies, it is interesting that the majority of studies report a reduction in hunger over periods of up to 24 hours after a fibre pre-load[19,17,20,10] or over periods of between one week and three months on a fibre supplemented diet.[21,22,23,24,13] This effect did not seem to depend on whether the fibre was consumed as tablets or granules of an isolated fibre source, as fibre supplemented foods or as the 'intact' fibre in naturally occurring foods. However, it did seem to vary between different types of fibre. Krotkiewski[24] showed that ingestion of 10 g of guar gum before meals reduced hunger scores in 21 obese volunteers to a significantly greater extent than did pre-meal supplements of 10 g of wheat bran. Unfortunately, most of these studies failed to monitor energy intake and in some of the hunger rating scale used was not properly validated. Predictions of the influence of these reported decreases in hunger on actual energy intakes are, therefore, impossible. It would appear that, although some types of dietary fibre can suppress hunger in obese individuals if given in sufficient quantities, the claim that this will facilitate a reduction in their energy consumption remains unsubstantiated.

DIETARY FIBRE AND ENERGY AVAILABILITY

It has been suggested that dietary fibre can help to achieve weight loss because 'a larger proportion of the calories will remain undigested'.[4] The considerable data on the effects of dietary fibre on nutrient digestion and absorption suggest that it reduces the availability of carbohydrates, fats and proteins in the diet and that some forms of fibre are more effective than others.[25,26,27]

Soluble fibres are generally thought to be most effective at reducing the glycaemic response to carbohydrate meals[28] although wheat bran has been shown to impair starch absorption[29] and to exert a small hypoglycaemic effect[30,28] in healthy volunteers. Faecal fat and nitrogen levels rose significantly in healthy subjects following a 16 g per day increase in fibre consumption from fruit and vegetables[31] and after a 28 g per day increase in fibre consumption from cereal sources.[32] Dietary supplementation with 36 g per day pectin[33] or 16 g per day cellulose[34] also increased faecal fat losses in man. These data are relevant to the study of obesity since they suggest a possible loss of available dietary energy to man.

Southgate and Durnin[35] reported a rise of 44–89 kcal per day in the faecal energy excretion of healthy subjects following an increased intake of fruit, vegetables and wholemeal bread (the fibre intake rose by about 10 g per day). In a later study, a 16 g per day increase in total fibre consumption, provided as fruit and vegetables, was shown to increase the faecal energy excretion in man by 138 kcal per day.[31] However, recent evidence suggests that undigested starch and dietary fibre, particularly soluble types, are metabolised by human colonic bacteria to short chain fatty acids which can then be absorbed.[36] Little

40

TABLE 2. Effects of dietary fibre on hunger sensation in man over periods of up to 24 hours

Authors	Fibre	Dose (g)	Administration	Subjects	Duration	Control	Hunger
Haber et al.[19]	Apple fibre	14	Whole apple	Lean	1 meal	Apple puree Apple juice	Reduced
Durrant & Royston[46]	Methyl-cellulose	1*	Soup, milkshake or sandwich pre-load	Obese	1 meal	Unsupplemented soup, milkshake sandwich	No effect
Wilmshurst & Crawley[17]	Guar gum	2*	Milky drink	Obese	1 meal	Unsupplemented milky drink	Reduced
Bolton et al.[20]	Grape, Orange fibre	4–16	Whole fruit	Lean	1 meal	Fruit juice	Reduced
Porikos & Hagamen[10]	Methyl-cellulose	7	High fibre sandwich	Obese Lean	1 meal	Low fibre sandwich	Reduced
Burley et al.[9]	Wheat bran + guar gum	12	Branflakes + guar bread	Lean	1 meal	Cornflakes + white bread (3 g DF)	No effect on hunger. Greater fullness

*Weight of supplement.

TABLE 3. Effects of dietary fibre on hunger sensation in man over 1–12 week periods

Authors	Fibre	Dose (g/day)	Administration	Subjects	Duration (weeks)	Control	Hunger
Shearer[21]	Methyl-cellulose + Alginic acid	2	Tablets before and between meals	Obese	2	Unsupplemented period	Reduced
Mickelsen et al.[22]	Cellulose	26 (CF)	High fibre bread	Obese	8	Low fibre bread (1 g CF/day)	Reduced
Hylander & Rossner[23]	Wheat bran or Ispaghula	7*	Bran or Ispaghula granules before meals	Obese	3	Unsupplemented group	Reduced by both fibres
Krotkiewski[24]	Guar gum or wheat bran	20*	Bran or guar granules before meals	Obese	3	None	Greater reduction with guar than bran
Rossner et al.[42]	Mixed grain + citrus fibre	5	Tablets before meals	Obese	8	Cornstarch and sucrose tablets (<1 g DF/day)	No effect
Rossner et al.[42]	Mixed grain, citrus + veg. fibre	7	Tablets before meals	Obese	12	Cornstarch and sucrose tablets (<1 g DF/day)	Tendency to reduce
Rigaud et al.[13]	Mixed grain, citrus + veg. fibre	7	Tablets before meals	Lean	4	Starch and lactose tablets (<1 g DF/day)	Reduced

*Weight of supplement.
CF = Crude fibre.

is known about the importance of these short chain fatty acids to man but it is thought that they represent a source of utilizable energy.[37] Any discussion of the effects of fibre on the available dietary energy in man must, therefore, consider the implication of fermentation processes in the colon.

Studies on mixed diets of varying cereal fibre content have shown that an increase in fibre consumption from 20 to 48 g per day provided an additional 227 kcal per day gross energy and increased the total energy losses via the faeces and urine by 156 kcal per day.[38] This difference in energy losses was mainly due to an increase in faecal energy excretion. The measured metabolisable energy (gross intake—faecal losses—urinary losses) of the high fibre diet in the above study was 4% greater than that of the low fibre diet. Earlier work reported that the provision of a very high fibre diet (85 g per day) supplied an extra 300 kcal per day gross energy, increased the faecal excretion of energy by 125 kcal per day and increased the metabolisable energy by 10%.[39] These results are consistent with the view that dietary fibre significantly contributes to the metabolisable energy.[3] Unfortunately, the increased fibre consumption in both studies mentioned was associated with a rise in intake of other energy supplying nutrients which themselves increased the gross energy intake and hence the metabolisable energy. Wisker *et al.*[38] calculated that, of the additional 227 kcal per day supplied by the high fibre diet, only 120 kcal could be attributed to the increased fibre intake *per se*. If the extra energy provided by non-fibre sources was removed from the calculation, a metabolisable energy value of 1825 kcal per day can be assigned to the high fibre diet. This represents a decrease in metabolisable energy of 2% when compared with the low fibre diet and supports the belief that the increased faecal losses of energy containing nutrients override any contribution of the fibre *per se* to the metabolisable energy of the diet.[40,41] In conclusion, it appears that the net effect of fibre associated faecal energy losses and energy gains via colonic fermentation of fibre remains unclear but that any change in the available dietary energy is unlikely to be large enough to be important in the management of obesity.

DIETARY FIBRE AND BODY WEIGHT

Since the primary goal in the treatment of obesity is to achieve an adequate reduction in body fat content, and hence in body weight, over the long term, any beneficial role of dietary fibre might be expected to improve weight loss or help maintain a lower body weight in the post-obese. Data on the effects of dietary fibre on body weight change in obese subjects are summarised in Table 4.

When pre-meal fibre supplements supplying between 6 and 7 g dietary fibre per day were taken together with a hypocaloric diet for periods of about 3 months, obese subjects lost between 1.6 and 2.1 kg more body weight than did controls given the same dietary advice but together with low fibre, placebo supplements.[42,43,44] In an earlier study guar gum or methylcellulose pre-meal supplements providing 10 g of fibre per day were suggested to improve weight

43

TABLE 4. Effect of dietary fibre on weight loss in obese patients

Authors	Fibre	Dose (g DF/day)	Administration	Duration (weeks)	Control	Weight change (kg)
Effects of pre-meal supplements:						
Evans & Miller[11]	Guar gum or Methyl-cellulose	10	Granules	1	Unsupplemented period	Guar = −1.5 Methyl-cellulose = −1.8
Hylander & Rossner[23]	Wheat bran or Ispaghula	7*	Bran or Ispaghula granules	2	Unsupplemented group	Bran = −4.6 Ispaghula = −4.2 Controls = −4.6
Krotkiewski[24] Walsh et al.[46]	Guar gum Glucomannan	20* 3*	Granules Capsules	8 8	None Starch capsules	Guar = −4.3 Glucomannan = −10.4 Control = +1.1 (P<0.005)
Rossner et al.[42]	Mixed grain, citrus+veg. fibre	7	Tablets	12	Cornstarch + glucose tablets (<1 g DF/day)	Fibre = −6.2 Control = −4.1 (P<0.05)
Solum et al.[43]	Mixed cereal+ citrus fibre	6	Tablets	12	Placebo tablets (1 g DF/day)	Fibre = −8.5 Control = −6.7 (P<0.01)
Stevens et al.[12]	Wheat bran, Psyllium gum or both	23	Crackers	2	Low fibre crackers (4 g DF/day)	No effect of fibre
Ryttig et al.[44]	Mixed Insol: Sol=10:1	7	Tablets	11	Placebo tablets	Fibre = −4.9 Control = −3.3 (P<0.05)
Effect of high fibre foods:						
Mickelsen et al.[22]	Cellulose	25	Bread with meals	8	Unsupplemented bread (1 g DF/day)	Cellulose = −8.8 Control = −6.3 (P<0.05)
Russ & Atkinson[45]	Mixed fibre	24	As part of high fibre diet	8	Low fibre diet	Fibre = −3.1 Control = −3.7

*Weight of supplement

loss in obese and lean subjects by reducing their energy intake below that reported when supplements were not taken.[11] However, these differences in weight loss were not shown statistically and were over a period of only 1 week. An uncontrolled study by Krotkiewski[24] reported a significant mean weight loss of 4.3 kg in a group of obese volunteers fed 10 g of a granulated guar gum preparation twice daily before meals for 8 weeks. These data were not confirmed when 6.6 g of wheat bran or ispaghula were consumed before meals for 2 weeks.[23]

Data on the weight changes in obese subjects when fibre is ingested in the form of fibre supplemented foods also appear confusing. Whereas 25 g of dietary fibre per day provided as cellulose supplemented bread produced an 8.8 kg weight loss over 8 weeks and unsupplemented break (1 g dietary fibre per day) only 6.3 kg over the same time period,[22] a similar level of fibre (23 g per day) but provided as wheat bran, psyllium gum, or wheat bran plus psyllium gum crackers failed to show a significant effect of fibre on weight loss.[12] Russ and Atkinson[45] compared the effects of a high fibre (24 g per day) and low fibre (13 g per day) diet on weight loss in obese subjects over an 8 week period. Mean weight losses at the end of the study were not significantly different between the two groups and it was suggested that the failure of the high fibre group to achieve the prescribed level of 45–50 g of fibre per day meant that their fibre intake was insufficient to produce the postulated beneficial effects on weight loss.

Data on the effect of dietary fibre on weight maintenance in the post-obese are few. Ryttig et al.[44] showed that a group of mildly obese subjects maintained a weight loss of 7 kg for 52 weeks when consuming 6 g of dietary fibre (mainly insoluble) per day. They did not monitor an unsupplemented control group over this period.

CONCLUSIONS

If given in sufficient quantity, some types of fibre appear to suppress hunger in obese subjects in the short term; as yet the long term effects on hunger remain unknown. Unfortunately, there is little evidence to suggest that fibre induced reductions in hunger sensation would reduce the total energy consumption. Although a high fibre diet increases faecal energy losses, undigested starch and dietary fibre, particularly soluble types, can be fermented in the colon and represent a potential source of energy to man. The net effect of fibre on available dietary energy to man is unclear but is unlikely to be large enough to be important in the treatment of obesity. If an appropriate loss of body weight is taken to indicate the success of obesity treatment, any therapeutic benefit of dietary fibre appears uncertain. Since short term effects on energy balance are of little consequence in the management of obesity, more controlled studies of the effect of different types of dietary fibre on weight loss in obese patients over several months are needed.

Benefits associated with an increased intake of dietary fibre have been reviewed by other speakers in this symposium, and of course these benefits apply also to obese people. However, current evidence indicates that dietary fibre has only a minor role to play in the prevention or treatment of obesity itself.

REFERENCES

1 Trowell H. Obesity in the Western world. *Plant Foods Man* 1975;**1**:157–9.
2 Leeds A R. Dietary fibre: Mechanisms of action. *Int J Obesity* 1987;**11**:Suppl. 1, 3–7.
3 Cummings J H. Dietary fibre. *Br Med Bull* 1981;**37**:65–70.
4 Eyton A. The F-plan diet. Harmondsworth: Penguin, 1982.
5 Heaton K W. Food fibre as an obstacle to energy intake. *Lancet* 1973;**2**:1418–21.
6 Van Itallie T B. Dietary fibre and obesity. *Am J Clin Nutr* 1978;**31**:S43–S52.
7 Grimes D S, Gordon C. Satiety value of white and wholemeal bread. *Lancet* 1978; **2**,106.
8 Bryson E, Dore C, Garrow J S. Wholemeal bread and satiety. *J Hum Nutr* 1980;**34**: 113–16.
9 Burley V J, Leeds A R, Blundell J E. The effect of high and low-fibre breakfasts on hunger, satiety and food intake in a subsequent meal. *Int J Obesity* 1987;**11**: Suppl. 1,87–93.
10 Porikos K, Hagamen S. Is fibre satiating? Effects of a high fibre preload on subsequent food intake of normal-weight and obese young men. *Appetite* 1986;**7**: 153–62.
11 Evans E, Miller D S. Bulking agents in the treatment of obesity. *Nutr Metabol* 1975; **18**:199–203.
12 Stevens J, Levitsky D A, Van Soest P J, Robertson J B, Kalkwarf H J, Roe D A. Effect of psyllium gum and wheat bran on spontaneous energy intake. *Am J Clin Nutr* 1987;**46**:812–17.
13 Rigaud D, Ryttig K R, Leeds A R, Bard D, Apfelbaum M. Effects of a moderate dietary fibre supplement on hunger rating, energy input and faecal energy output in young, healthy volunteers: a randomised, double-blind cross-over trial. *Int J Obesity* 1987;**11**:Suppl. 1,73–8.
14 Kahaner N, Fuchs H M, Floch M H. The effect of dietary fibre supplementation in man. 1. Modification of eating habits. *Am J Clin Nutr* 1976;**29**:1437–42.
15 Duncan K H, Bacon J A, Weinsier R L. The effects of high and low energy density diets on satiety, energy intake, and eating time of obese and nonobese subjects. *Am J Clin Nutr* 1983;**37**:763–7.
16 Blundell J E, Burley V J. Satiation, satiety and the action of fibre on food intake. *Int J Obesity* 1987;**11**:Suppl. 1,9–25.
17 Wilmshurst P, Crawley J C W. The measurement of gastric transit time in obese subjects using Na and the effects of energy content and guar gum on gastric emptying and satiety. *Br J Nutr* 1980;**44**:1–6.
18 Castonguay T W, Applegate E A, Upton D E, Stern J S. Hunger and appetite: old concepts/new distinctions. *Nutr Rev* 1983;**41**:101–10.
19 Haber G B, Heaton K W, Murphy D, Burroughs L. Depletion and disruption of dietary fibre. Effects on satiety, plasma-glucose and serum-insulin. *Lancet* 1977; **2**,679–82.
20 Bolton R P, Heaton K W, Burroughs L F. The role of dietary fibre in satiety, glucose and insulin: studies with fruit and fruit juice. *Am J Clin Nutr* 1981;**34**: 211–17.

21 Shearer R S. Effects of bulk-producing tablets on hunger intensity in dieting patients. *Curr Ther Res* 1976;**19**:433–41.

22 Mickelsen O, Makdani D D, Cotton R H, Titcomb S T, Colmey J C, Gatty R. Effects of a high fibre bread diet on weight loss in college-age males. *Am J Clin Nutr* 1979;**32**:1703–9.

23 Hylander B, Rossner S. Effects of dietary fibre intake before meals on weight loss and hunger in a weight-reducing club. *Acta Med Scand* 1983;**213**:217–20.

24 Krotokiewski M. Effect of guar gum on body-weight, hunger ratings and metabolism in obese subjects. *Br J Nutr* 1984;**52**:97–105.

25 Cummings J H. Nutritional implications of dietary fibre. *Am J Clin Nutr* 1978;**31**: S21–S29.

26 Leeds A R. Modification of intestinal absorption by dietary fibre and fibre components. In: Vahouny G V and Kritchevsky D (eds) *Dietary fibre in health and disease*, pp. 53–71. New York: Plenum Publishing Co., 1982.

27 Vahouny C V, Cassidy M M. Dietary fibres and absorption of nutrients. *Proc Soc Exp Biol Med* 1985;**180**:432–46.

28 Jenkins D J A, Wolever T M S, Leeds A R, Gassull M A, Haisman P, Dilawari J, Goff D V, Metz G L, Alberti K G M M. Dietary fibres, fibre analogues and glucose tolerance, importance of viscosity. *Br Med J* 1978;**1**:1392–4.

29 Hamberg O, Rumessen J J, Gudmand-Hoyer E. Inhibition of starch absorption by dietary fibre. *Scand J Gastroenterol* 1989;**24**:103–9.

30 Jefferys D B. The effect of dietary fibre on the response to orally administered glucose. *Proc Nutr Soc.* 1974;**33**:11A.

31 Kelsay J L, Behall K M, Prather E S. Effect of fibre from fruits and vegetables on metabolic responses of human subjects. 1. Bowel transit time, number of defaecations, faecal weight, urinary excretions of energy and nitrogen and apparent digestibilities of energy nitrogen and fat. *Am J Clin Nutr* 1978;**31**: 1149–53.

32 Cummings J H, Hill M J, Jenkins D J A, Pearson J R, Wiggins H S. Changes in faecal composition and colonic function due to cereal fibre. *Am J Clin Nutr* 1976;**29**:1468–73.

33 Cummings J H, Southgate D A T, Branch W J, Wiggins, H S, Houston H, Jenkins D. J. A, Jibraj T, Hill N W. The digestion of dietary pectin in the human gut, and its effect on calcium absorption and large bowel function. *Br J Nutr* 1979;**41**: 477–85.

34 Slavin J L, Marlett J A. Effect of refined cellulose on apparent energy, fat and nitrogen digestibilities. *J Nutr* 1980;**110**:2020–6.

35 Southgate D A T, Durnin J V G A. Calorie conversion factors. An experimental reassessment of the factors used in the calculation of the energy value of human diets. *Br J Nutr* 1970;**24**:517–35.

36 Fleming L L, Floch M H. Digestion and absorption of fibre carbohydrate in the colon. *Am J Gastroenterol* 1986;**81**:507–11.

37 Cummings J H. Fermentation in the human large intestine: evidence and implications for health. *Lancet* 1983;**1**:1206–9.

38 Wisker E, Maltz A, Feldheim W. Metabolisable energy of diets low or high in dietary fibre from cereals when eaten by humans. *J Nutr* 1988;**118**:945–52.

39 Goranzon H, Forsum E, Thilen M. Calculation and determination of metabolizable energy in mixed diets to humans. *Am J Clin Nutr* 1983;**38**:954–63.

40 Southgate D A T. Fibre and other unavailable carbohydrates and their effects on the energy value of the diet. *Proc Nutr Soc* 1973;**32**:131–6.

41 Miles C W, Kelsay J L, Wong N P. Effect of dietary fibre on the metabolisable energy of human diets. *J Nutr* 1988;**118**:1075–81.
42 Rossner S, Von Zweigbergk D, Ohlin A, Ryttig K. Weight reduction with dietary fibre supplements. Results of two double-blind randomised studies. *Acta Med Scand* 1987;**222**:83–8.
43 Solum T T, Ryttig K R, Solum E, Larsen S. The influence of a high-fibre diet on body weight, serum lipids and bloud pressure in slightly overweight persons: A randomised, double-blind, placebo-controlled investigation with diet and fibre tablets (Dumo Vital). *Int J Obesity* 1987;**11**:Suppl. 1,67–71.
44 Ryttig K R, Tellnes G, Haegh L, Boe E, Fagerthun H. A dietary fibre supplement and weight maintenance after weight reduction: A randomised, double-blind, placebo controlled long-term trial. *Int J Obesity* 1989;**13**:165–71.
45 Russ C S, Atkinson R L. Use of high fibre diets for the outpatient treatment of obesity. *Nutr Rep Int* 1985;**32**:193–8.
46 Walsh D E, Yaghoubian V, Behforooz A. Effect of glucomannan on obese patients: A clinical study. *Int J Obesity* 1984;**8**:289–93.
47 Durrant M L, Royston P. The effect of preloads of varying energy density and methyl cellulose on hunger, appetite and salivation. *Proc Nutr Soc* 1978;**37**:87A.

DISCUSSION

Prof Bloom   What would be the weight reduction effect of nuisance factors, such as a screaming baby during eating, as well as having to stuff masses into your mouth? What sort of comparator ought to be used here?

Prof Garrow   One of the problems about doing trials on weight loss induced by fibre is that it is impossible to do them double blind. Anyone who is having a high fibre intake knows about it. If they happen to believe passionately that fibre is good stuff, it is then impossible to sort out the rather powerful psychological effect.

Dr Eastwood   Do you think the decreases in weight on low fibre diets are in part due to an emptying of the colon, due to a decrease in both dietary and bacterial intraluminal mass? Secondly, why in the light of your figures, do you think F plan proved to be so successful?

Prof Garrow   I said that I thought that it was rightly a very popular book. The book shops are full of 'no-diet weight-loss' books, suggesting that if you think pure thoughts or something, weight will fall off you. What Audrey Eyton did was that she perfectly correctly quoted the principles of energy balance, pointed out that it was necessary to eat fewer calories than you expend and said—possibly correctly—that a high fibre diet made it easier to do so. Although the evidence for that last bit was a little bit dodgy, it does not prevent this in my opinion from being still by far the best of the popular diet books. The evidence that fibre supplements or high fibre foods produce weight loss is pretty poor. Nevertheless, from the range of diet books available, it is not surprising that hers is so successful.

As to your first question, clearly, in the short term, if you change from a low fibre to a high fibre diet, there is an initial weight gain due to the increase gut filling. If you are talking about long-term, 52 weeks changes, then the sort of weight loss that you expect to get in that period would overwhelm that relatively small effect. Perhaps you can tell me what the weight of gut contents is?

Prof Read   Is there any evidence to support the idea that the more you chew food the less you will eat? I, like you, do not think it is due to getting tired, but I have heard people say, 'Perhaps chewing causes afferent signals to go to the brain that affect the eating centre. Does chewing gum have any effect on eating behaviour?

Prof Garrow   Advice has been given as part of behaviour therapy, that people who wish to lose weight should eat slowly. This has been shown to produce weight loss. People who are trying to diet frequently forget that they have eaten, especially if they happen to have been watching the television set at the same time. I do not know of any good studies in which chewing alone, or differences in chewing pattern have been related to satiety.

FIBRE: DO WE NEED IT?
THE ROLE OF FIBRE IN THE COLON; BULKING AND MOTILITY

Professor N W Read
Royal Hallamshire Hospital
Sheffield

HOW DOES FIBRE WORK ON THE COLON?

Wheat bran and other bulk laxatives containing complex polysaccharides are not digested in the small intestine, but act on the colon to increase stool weight and frequency, to make the stool softer and bulkier and to reduce whole gut transit time.[1,2]

The mechanism of the laxative action of bran and other types of fibre on the colon is not established. They are thought to act by increasing the bulk of the colonic contents. The increased colonic bulk then probably promotes[3] colonic propulsion which leads to reduced water absorption by the colon and the passage of larger and softer stools, which are easier to evacuate.[4]

The increased colonic bulk may result from several mechanisms

(i) Fibre contains plant cell walls that may resist breakdown by bacteria; and the associated complex polysaccharides adsorb and retain water.
(ii) Complex polysaccharides also stimulate microbial cell growth, resulting in a greater faecal bacterial cell mass.
(iii) Fermentation of complex polysaccharides releases gases which may be trapped in colonic contents contributing to their bulk and plasticity.

In a recent study comparing the action of a number of complex polysaccharides with their fermentation characteristics, Tomlin[5] has suggested that polysaccharides that resisted breakdown increased stool weight, while those that were fermented, accelerated colonic transit. The best bulk laxatives appeared to be those, like bran and ispaghula, that retained their structure but were also fermented.

There may be other mechanisms of action. It is possible, for example, that the lignified particles of bran irritate the colonic epithelium, activating nervous reflexes that cause colonic secretion and propulsion. This may explain why coarse bran is a more potent laxative than the same amount of finely milled bran.[6] In support of this idea, Tomlin and Read have recently observed[7] that the addition of 15 g/day of small segments of polyvinyl tubing to the diet increases stool mass and frequency, improves stool consistency and accelerates whole gut transit to the same extent as the addition of an equivalent weight of coarse wheat bran. Table 1.

An interesting study from Italy[8] showed that treatment of severe painless constipation with bran restored the reduced anal relaxation in response to

TABLE 1.

	Control	Plastic	Bran
Weekly stool mass (kg)	1.06	1.35*	1.56*
Weekly stool frequency	6.9	8.3	9.1
Mean stool consistency 1	5.6	5.1	5.1
Whole gut transit time (hours) 2	54.2	38.2	42.3*

*Indicates significant difference compared with control.
1, scale from 1 to 8.
2, transit time value is the median of seven daily values for each volunteer using continuous method.

rectal distension, but not the blunted rectal sensitivity. The mechanism of this novel finding is fascinating. Do the products of fermentation or the particulate nature of the bran modulate responses to colonic distension? Or does the ready expulsion of the faeces allow the stretch receptors to re-adapt to lower rectal volumes?

IS CONSTIPATION A DISEASE OF FIBRE DEFICIENCY?

The observation that population groups taking a high-fibre diet had a larger 24 h faecal output and more rapid gastrointestinal transit than groups taking a low fibre diet[2] popularised the view that constipation in the British population is mainly caused by fibre deficiency. More recent studies within Britain and USA have shown that variation in fibre intake is indeed a determinant of stool output but not necessarily the most important one. If vegans and vegetarians are included in the population sample, then there is a very strong correlation between fibre intake and stool output ($r = 0.96$ in 51 subjects studied).[9] In a more normal population sample, the correlation between fibre intake and 7 day stool weight is quite weak ($r = 0.41$)[10] while in America, in volunteers kept in a metabolic ward, psychological factors accounted for as much variance in stool output as did dietary fibre intake—extroverts having bigger stools than introverts.[11] This may explain why, when normal people are given the same strictly controlled intake of fibre, their 24 hour stool weight varies over a three fold range[12] or possibly even more.[13]

The word constipation means different things to different people[14] and people who complain of constipation do not necessarily pass less faeces than their fellows.[15] It is not surprising, therefore, that the fibre intake of constipated people[16,17] may be less, the same, or even more than that of controls, especially as some of them will have tried to help themselves by eating more fibre-rich foods. Meta-analysis of the data from 20 studies[18] showed that stool output and transit times responded less to fibre supplementation in constipated patients than in normal subjects, and failed to demonstrate that treatment with fibre could return transit time and stool output to normal.

There is therefore little evidence to support the contention that constipation in all patients is wholly caused by fibre deficiency, and constipated patients should not be blamed for non-compliance if dietary advice fails. Constipation should probably be regarded as a disorder of colonic or anorectal motility that may respond to the mild laxative action of complex polysaccharides rather than simply the result of a fibre deficient diet.[19]

IS FIBRE USEFUL IN CONSTIPATION?

The majority of patients with mild or moderate constipation probably benefit from treatment with wheat bran or viscous polysaccharides such as ispaghula. In particular, elderly constipated patients often ingest a diet lower in fibre content than their non-constipated peers and often find fibre supplements helpful in achieving normal bowel action. Nevertheless, not all patients with constipation respond to treatment with dietary fibre. Patients with neuropathic constipation[18] obtain little benefit from bran or other bulking agents such as ispaghula; most patients are already ingesting a large amount of dietary fibre and find that bran had no effect or made their symptoms worse.

IS FIBRE EFFECTIVE IN IRRITABLE BOWEL SYNDROME?
What is Irritable Bowel Syndrome?

Irritable Bowel Syndrome (IBS) is characterised by an alteration in bowel habit which may either be diarrhoea or constipation and abdominal discomfort or pain. Since routine clinical investigations fail to identify a cause, IBS is often a diagnosis of exclusion. Manning and Heaton have attempted to identify the positive discriminative symptoms for IBS,[20] but many of these features are shared by patients with inflammatory bowel disease,[21] and may in any case only identify a subset of the disease.

There is no general agreement about the pathogenesis of IBS or how it should be categorised. Some insights may be gained from a careful history. Since patients perceptions of both diarrhoea and constipation vary considerably, it is important to ask more detailed questions about bowel habit. A large proportion of patients complain of symptoms such as a frequent desire to defaecate, a feeling of incomplete evacuation, abdominal pain relieved by defaecation, and urgency. These patients may present with either constipation or diarrhoea. Such symptoms are suggestive of rectal irritability and are shared by patients with inflammatory bowel disease and solitary rectal ulcer syndrome.[22,23] They are often associated with upper gut symptoms such as feelings of early satiety, nausea, and bloating after meals.[24] This subset of IBS may represent the common end result of a number of pathophysiological processes, some of which affect just the lower bowel, some the whole gastrointestinal tract. Emotional tension is commonly considered to be the most important aetiological factor but other possible factors include bile acid malabsorption, impaired gut permeability with activation of immunoreactive cells, and subclinical gastrointestinal inflammation.

The patients with this subset of IBS show exaggerated rectal motor responses to distension,[25,26] ingestion of a meal, stress and cholecystokinin. Similar exaggerated responses to stimuli have been reported in the ileum.[27] The hyper-reactive bowel is also abnormally sensitive to distension.[25]

Patients who present with constipation and abdominal bloating and pain often do not have features of rectal irritability and should perhaps be categorised in a different subset. The most severely affected patients in this subset have a disturbance in the function of the enteric nervous system and a mild form of chronic intestinal pseudo-obstruction.[28]

Other patients may complain of diarrhoea, pain and excessive flatulence caused by over-consumption or impaired absorption of carbohydrate.[29] Some may be intolerant to wheat and others may be consuming too much fibre.

For the purpose of therapeutic trials, patients with widely different presenting features (the sole commonality being the failure of the physician to find a cause for the symptoms) are lumped together and the effect of treatment is often gauged only on the basis of global symptomatic responses. It is not surprising that no effective treatment for this condition has emerged, though some would claim that psychotherapy helps most patients.

Treatment of IBS with wheat bran

The popularity of wheat bran as a natural way to manage IBS has made it the first line treatment for this condition for over 10 years.[1] But is it an effective treatment for IBS? Manning and Heaton showed that the addition of 7 grams of fibre in the form of wheat bran for 6 weeks to the diet of patients with IBS resulted in significant improvement in symptoms.[30] The possibility that the control diet in Manning and Heaton's study had little placebo effect[31] make the results of the bran diet difficult to interpret in a condition that shows such a marked response to placebos.[32] Other placebo controlled trials of bran in IBS[32,33,34,35] have failed to show any convincing effect of the fibre on overall symptom patterns. The most recent study[35] compared the effect of supplementing the daily diet of 44 IBS patients with either 12 bran biscuits (12.8 grams fibre) or 12 placebo biscuits (2.5 grams fibre). Patients were randomly allocated to receive either high fibre or placebo biscuits for 3 months and then to cross over to the alternative biscuit for another three months. The patients were not told which type of biscuits they had been given, though some may have guessed! The results showed that both placebo and bran groups experienced similar improvements in overall symptom scores. Moreover the beneficial effects of bran were independent of any change in stool weight. The paucity of constipated patients may have influenced the conclusions from this study.

Cann and colleagues[32] compared the independent responses of a number of typical IBS symptoms to bran and placebo tablets in 38 patients. Eighteen patients (47%) said they had improved on bran treatment, but only five of these said that they were entirely satisfied and did not require further treatment. Eleven patients (29%) experienced no change in their symptoms, and

TABLE 2.

Authors	IBS or DD	Numbers of patients' controls	Age of patients (mean or median range)	Fibre	Duration of treatment	Effect of fibre vs control	Comments
Soltoft et al.[33]	IBS + DD	29,23	40 (18–73)	Fine bran 30 g day^{-1} in biscuits	6 weeks	No difference in overall assessment nor in days with pain	No laxative effect of bran apparent. Placebo biscuits had marked effect
Manning et al.[30]	IBS	13,11	20–60	Fine bran 20 g day^{-1}, or equivalent wholemeal bread	6 weeks	Pain less severe and less frequent. Bowel habit improved. Less mucus passed	Colonic motor activity reduced by bran. Placebo was dummy diet sheet, had little effect
Cann et al.[32]	IBS	38,28	32 (19–61)	Coarse bran 20 g day^{-1}	4 weeks	No difference in any symptoms except constipation	Placebo tablets had marked effect. Bran always given first. Full dose taken only 1 or 2 weeks
Richie & Truelove[39]	IBS	12,12	38 (16–69)	Ispaghula (Fybogel) 7 g day^{-1}	3 months	Overall improvement only on active agent (in 5 of 12 patients)	Placebo powder had no effect

Study	Type	Number	Age	Treatment	Duration	Results	Comments
Longstreth et al.[42]	IBS + DD	26,34	38	Psyllium (Metamucil) 10.8 g day^{-1}	8 weeks	No difference in pain improvement or overall improvement	Placebo powder had marked effect but also relieved constipation
Arthurs & Fielding[43]	IBS	80	28	Ispaghula	4 weeks	No effect on overall improvement	
Lucey et al.[35]	IBS	28 (crossover)	—	Bran biscuits (15 g fibre)	6 months	No difference despite an increase in stool weight on bran	—
Kumar et al.[41]	IBS	14,10		Ispaghula (30 g)		Significant improvement in symptoms including diarrhoea, increased stool weight. No change in transit time	Only anal patients. No placebo study due in India
Prior & Whorwell[40]	IBS	80	18–63	Ispaghula 10.9 g/day	12 weeks	Global assessment better on ispaghula than placebo. Improvement in constipation. No change in diarrhoea	

nine patients (24%) found that their symptoms were exacerbated by a high fibre diet. When the characteristics of the patients who said they had improved on bran were compared with those who said that their symptoms had not changed or become worse, the bran responders had smaller, harder, less frequent stools and longer colonic transit times upon entering the trial than the non-responders. In other words, it was the more constipated patients that responded to bran. This impression was confirmed by analysis of the responses to individual symptoms; constipation was the only symptom that showed a significantly greater response to bran than placebo. This does not mean that none of the other symptoms responded to bran. They did, but the responses were no greater than the responses to placebo. This study failed to confirm the suggestion that ingestion of wheat bran in patients with diarrhoea delays rapid intestinal transit.[36,37] Instead, wheat bran tended to accelerate transit in everybody and exacerbate symptoms of diarrhoea.

So is there any point in advising patients to take bran for their irritable guts? The idea should not be rejected completely, but a sense of realism is needed. Some IBS patients, particularly those who are constipated, undoubtedly obtain symptomatic relief from taking bran in their diet and should continue to do so. Others find that bran induces or exacerbates symptoms of distension, flatulence, diarrhoea and abdominal pain. Their hypersensitive and irritable guts are probably irritated by the particulate nature of the bran, its bulk and the products of its fermentation by colonic bacteria. In the current climate of bran for everything, judicious reduction in fibre intake in these patients can prove very useful. For the remainder then, bran is a less toxic 'placebo' than many drugs[38] and is better than placebo for constipation associated with IBS.

Viscous polysaccharides

Are other types of complex polysaccharide more effective in the management of constipation? Ritchie and Truelove[39] showed that ispaghula was better than wheat bran when both were given in combination with a psychotropic agent and an antispasmodic. In a large controlled trial, published last year,[40] Prior and Whorwell reported overall symptomatic improvement in 82% patients, who had been taking ispaghula compared with 53% patients who had been taking placebo. Many of their patients had constipation and in these ispaghula accelerated transit time and increased stool weight. There was no evidence that ispaghula improved patients with diarrhoea.

Kumar and his colleagues[41] carried out a dose ranging study in a group of male Asian patients to determine the optimum dose of ispaghula husk in IBS and to assess the correlation between the relief in patients' symptoms and colonic function. Thirty grams of ispaghula caused a significant improvement in patients' symptoms, accompanied by an increase in stool weight but no significant change in transit time. Surprisingly, patients reported improvement in diarrhoea, even though stool weight increased.

The results of previous trials of bran and viscous polysaccharides in IBS are summarised in Table 2.

CONCLUSION

It seems likely that complex polysaccharides will only benefit subsets of patients with IBS and idiopathic constipation. Therapy can only be effective when we have agreed on how these subsets can be identified.

REFERENCES

1 Manning A P, Heaton K W. Bran and the irritable bowel syndrome. *Lancet* 1976;**i**: 588.

2 Burkitt D P, Walker A R P, Painter N S. Effect of dietary fibre on stools and transit times, and its role in the causation of disease. *Lancet* 1972;**ii**:1408–12.

3 Chauve A, Devroede G, Bastin E. Intraluminal pressure during perfusion of the human colon *in situ*. *Gastroenterology* 1976;**70**:336–44.

4 Bannister J J, Davison P, Timms J M, Gibbons C G, Read N W. Effect of the stool size and consistency of defaecation. *Gut* 1987;**28**:1246–50.

5 Tomlin J, Read N W. The relationship between bacterial degradation of fibre and stool output in man. *Br J Nutr* 1988;**60**:467–75.

6 Brodribb A J M, Groves C. Effect of bran particle size on stool weight. *Gut* 1978;**19**: 60–3.

7 Tomlin J, Read N W. Laxative effects of undigestible plastic particles. *Br Med J* 1988;**297**:1175–6.

8 Marzio L, Lanfranchi G A, Bazzochi G, Cuccurullo F. Anorectal motility and rectal sensitivity in chronic idiopathic constipation: effect of a high fibre diet. *J Clin Gastroenterol* 1985;**7**:391–9.

9 Davies G J, Crowder M, Reid B, Dickerson J W T. Bowel function measurements of individuals with different eating patterns. *Gut* 1986;**27**:164–9.

10 Eastwood M A, Brydon W G, Baird J D *et al*. Faecal weight and composition, serum lipids and diet among subjects aged 18–80 years not seeking health care. *Am J Clin Nutr* 1984;**40**:628–34.

11 Tucker D M, Sandstead H H, Logan G M *et al*. Dietary fiber and personality factors as determinants of stool output. *Gastroenterology* 1981;**81**:879–83.

12 Cummings J H, Southgate D A T, Branch W, Houston H, Jenkins D J A, James W P T. Colonic responses to dietary fibre from carrot, cabbage, apple, bran, and guar gum. *Lancet* 1978;**1**:5–9.

13 Stephen A M, Wiggins H S, Englyst H N, Cole T J, Wayman B J, Cummings J H. The effect of age, sex, and level of intake of dietary fibre from wheat on large-bowel function in thirty healthy subjects. *Br J Nutr* 1986;**56**:349–61.

14 Moore-Gillon V. Constipation: what does the patient mean? *J R Soc Med* 1984;**77**: 108–10.

15 Meyer F, Le Quintrec Y. Rapport entre fibres alimentaires et constipation. *Nouv Presse Med* 1981;**10**:2479–81.

16 Johnson C K, Kolasa K, Chenoweth W, Bennick M. Health, laxation, and food habit influences on fiber intake of older women. *J Am Diet Assoc* 1980;**77**: 551–7.

17 Preston D M, Lennard Jones J E. Severe chronic constipation of young women: 'idiopathic slow transit constipation'. *Gut* 1986;**27**:41–8.

18 Muller-Lissner S A. The effect of wheat bran on weight of stool and gastrointestinal transit time: a meta analysis. *Br Med J* 1988;**296**:615–17.

19 Cummings J H. Constipation, dietary fibre and control of large bowel function. *Postgrad Med J* 1984;**60**:811–19.

20 Manning A P, Thompson W G, Heaton K W, Morris A F. Towards a positive diagnosis of the irritable bowel. *Br Med J* 1978;**2**:653–4.

21 Thompson W G, Gastrointestinal symptoms in the irritable bowel compared with peptic ulcer and inflammatory bowel disorder. *Gut* 1984;**25**:1089–92.

22 Rao S S C, Holdsworth C D, Read N W. Symptoms and stool patterns in patients with ulcerative colitis. *Gut* 1988;**29**:342–5.

23 Sun W M, Read N W, Donnelly T C, Bannister J J, Shorthouse A J. A common pathophysiology for full thickness rectal prolapse, anterior mucosal prolapse and solitary rectal ulcer. *Br J Surg* 1989;**76**:In press.

24 Whorwell P J, McCallum M, Creed F H, Roberts C T, Non-colonic features of irritable bowel syndrome. *Gut* 1986;**27**:37–40.

25 Whitehead W E, Engle B T, Schuster M V. Irritable bowel syndrome. Physiological and psychological differences between diarrhoea-predominant and constipation-predominant patients. *Dig Dis Sci* 1980;**25**:404–13.

26 Almy T, Hinckle L, Berle B, Kern F. Alterations in colonic function under stress III. Experimental production of sigmoid spasm in patients with spastic complication. *Gastroenterology* 1949;**12**:437–39.

27 Kellow J E, Phillips S F. Altered small bowel motility in irritable bowel syndrome is correlated with symptoms. *Gastroenterology* 1987;**92**:1885–93.

28 Stanghellini V, Canilleri M, Malagelada J-R. Chronic idiopathic intestinal pseudo-obstruction: clinical and intestinal manometric findings. *Gut* 1987;**28**:5–12.

29 Rumessen J J, Gudmand-Mayer E. Functional bowel disease: Malabsorption and abdominal distress after ingestion of fructose sorbital and fructose sorbital mixtures. *Gastroenterology* 1988;**95**:694–700.

30 Manning A P, Heaton K W, Harvey R F, Uglow P. Wheat fibre and the irritable bowel syndrome. *Lancet* 1977;**i**:417–18.

31 Heaton K W. Role of dietary fibre in the treatment of irritable bowel syndrome. In: Read N W (ed.) *Irritable Bowel Syndrome*. Orlando, FL, Grune and Stratton, pp. 203–22: 1985.

32 Cann P A, Read N W, Holdsworth C D. What is the benefit of coarse wheat bran in patients with irritable bowel syndrome? *Gut* 1984;**24**:168–73.

33 Soltoft J, Gudman-Hoyer E, Krag B, Kristensen E, Wulfe M R. A double blind trial of the effect of wheat bran on symptoms of the irritable bowel syndrome. *Lancet* 1976;**ii**:270–2.

34 Arffman S, Anderson J R, Hegnhoj J *et al.* The effect of coarse wheat bran in the irritable bowel syndrome. A double blind cross over study. *Scand J Gastroenterol* 1985;**20**:295–8.

35 Lucey M R, Clark M L, Lowndes J O, Dawson A M. Is bran 8 efficacious in irritable bowel syndrome. A double blind cross over study. *Gut* 1987;**28**:221–5.

36 Harvey R F, Pomare E W, Heaton K W. Effects of increase dietary fibre on intestinal transit. *Lancet* 1973;**i**:1278–80.

37 Payler D K, Pomare E W, Heaton K W, Harvey R F. The effect of wheat bran on intestinal transit. *Gut* 1975;**16**:209–13.

38 Anon. Some antispasmodic drugs for the irritable bowel syndrome. *Drug Ther Bull* 1986;**24**:93–5.

39 Ritchie J A, Truelove S C. Treatment of irritable bowel syndrome with lorazepam, hyoscine butylbromide and ispaghula husk. *Br Med J* 1979;**1**:376–8.

40 Prior A, Whorwell P J. Double blind study of ispaghula in the irritable bowel syndome. *Gut* 1987;**28**:1510–13.

41 Kumar A, Kumar N, Vij J C *et al.* Optimum dosage of ispaghula husk in patients with irritable bowel syndrome—Correlation of symptom relief with whole gut transit time and stool weight. *Gut* 1987;**28**:150–5.
42 Longstreth G F, Fox D D, Youkeles L *et al.* Psyllium therapy in the irritable bowel syndrome: a double blind trial. *Ann Int Med* 1981;**95**:53–6.
43 Arthurs Y, Fielding J F. Double blind trial of ispaghula/poloxamer in the irritable bowel syndrome. *Int Med J* 1983;**76**:253–5.

DISCUSSION

Prof Bloom   You said that bran was the same as other bulking agents and that therefore it was a good treatment for constipation. Which bulking agent is the most effective has not really been tested and in the current climate needs testing on thousands of people to see whether they do actually cause the effect intended and what are the bad side effects. Because bran is a 'natural substance', one may prescribe it, perhaps to prevent colonic cancer, with little idea of the possible long-term side effects. So firstly, is bran the right agent, and secondly, what unexpected long-term side effects are there likely to be?

Prof Read   I do not know whether bran is the right or optimal agent. It is a useful way of increasing fibre intake in our patients, because it is something that is readily available. Perhaps some of the viscous agents, such as ispaghula, are more acceptable to patients than bran. I do not know whether ispaghula is actually more potent, but it certainly can be more acceptable, particularly if it is flavoured. Ken Heaton would say you should put everybody on a high fibre diet, but it is very difficult for people to actually comply with a high fibre diet without being given something as a medicine. As to long-term effects, again, I do not know. One is inclined to say, 'Well, if a high bran diet can be equated with the sort of diet that people eat in rural Africa, maybe there are no deleterious long-term effects.

Prof Bloom   In the drug industry that would be illegal, i.e. speculating that a drug is going to work because there is a good, rational reason. We used to do that sort of thing, such as giving anticoagulants for heart disease, until we discovered that people died of the anticoagulants and were not saved from heart disease. We now realise that we have to do double blind trials and look for side effects. Bran is an untested agent, and is not necessarily safe because it comes from artificially grown wheat, made in factories and packaged in bags.

Audience   Have you looked at exercise as well as diet in women with slow transit constipation?

Prof Read   Not systematically. I have advised many of these patients to take more exercise and do a variety of things, but it does not seem to help very much with this particular group. In people with milder forms of constipation it can help, but it does not help severe constipation. The mind is also important. I had one patient who was severely constipated and had been coming to my clinic for 2 years. She came in one afternoon looking smart and attractive. I said, 'You are looking marvellous this afternoon,' and she said, 'Well, I can defecate, I am cured.' I said, 'Why? There are 20 other people out there who cannot go and I do not know what to do with them.' She said, 'Well, a month ago I divorced my husband.'

Audience You seem to be advocating bran and talking about high fibre, but how much fluid are you recommending? From my experience a lot of constipation problems result from lack of fluid in the diet.

Prof Read Yes, that point was also made to me in Australia. People said, 'This is a summer disease,' and 'It could be due to fluid depletion.' I am afraid I do not advocate more fluid in their diet; maybe I should. I do not know of any strong evidence that relates fluid intake and stool output, though I suppose that if you are fluid depleted you will absorb more from the gut because of the effects of aldosterone and ADH.

FIBRE AND DIABETES

Dr Mike Lean
Senior Lecturer
University Department of Human Nutrition
Royal Infirmary
Glasgow

INTRODUCTION

Epidemiology and theory

Dietary fibre is of possible importance in both the aetiology of diabetes (NIDDM) and its treatment (both of IDDM and NIDDM). The link with the aetiology of NIDDM (Type 2 diabetes) arose from reports about its apparently low frequency in some primitive countries where the intakes of dietary fibre are high.[1] Additionally, higher rates of diabetes have been reported in migrant populations who adopt Western-style low fibre diets. A similar epidemiological argument relates the reduced incidence of diabetes in Europe during the world wars to the use of unrefined flour in bread and its higher dietary fibre content. At best, such evidence is circumstantial, and many other dietary and related lifestyle factors could be invoked as affecting diabetes rates. Doubt has been introduced because although the original observations in Uganda did relate to people with very high dietary fibre intakes, the diets in countries like Japan, supposed earlier to be high in dietary fibre, have recently been found by reliable survey work to contain similar amounts to Western diets.[2] Furthermore, with proper screening, prevalence of NIDDM has proved to be very high in many developing countries, although lower in traditional rural communities with high dietary fibre intakes.[3]

There is also a suggestion from the European wartime data, showing sharply reduced diabetes-mortality rates, that increased dietary fibre intakes (mainly from flour and bread whose intake rose 20% and whose dietary fibre content rose 3–4 times during the war) may exert a protective effect against ischaemic vascular disease.[1,4] This opens the question of the possible role of dietary fibre in the management of diabetes which forms the bulk of this paper. Mechanisms by which dietary fibre might affect development of NIDDM would be the same as those which operate in its management.

Interpretation of research in this field has often been confusing, not least because dietary fibre is a term used for a variety of chemical compounds (naturally occurring or purified) with different nutritional effects. Dietary fibre is a food component, and altering its intake through dietary manipulation necessarily involves changes in other nutrients, which may themselves modify gastrointestinal or metabolic functions. Thus the food sources of dietary fibre characteristically contain a lot of carbohydrate (both simple and complex in different foods), little fat, and often antinutrient lectins (in

61

TABLE 1.

Erroneous enthusiasm about dietary fibre

Use of vast test loads
Presence of other dietary factors
Placebo effect
Poor study design
Undetected negative energy balance

Erroneous dismissal of dietary fibre as ineffective

Inadequate group difference in fibre intake
Insufficient numbers to exclude beta errors
Poor study design
Undetected positive energy balance
Concentrating on cereal not viscous fibre
Basic diet too low in carbohydrate (< 50%)
Anti-placebo effect (prejudice)
Unpalatability causing non-compliance
Very poor diabetic control in subjects

TABLE 2.

Possible benefits of dietary fibre for diabetics

Hypoglycaemic
Prevent hypoglycaemia
Hypolipidaemic
Hypotensive
Weight loss
Reduce risks of macrovascular disease
Reduce risks of microvascular disease

---

legumes, pulses etc.). Many other sources of error have arisen in published studies (Table 1). One of the most widely quoted studies of high fibre diets in diabetes involved taking 42% of total energy as legumes (beans morning, noon and night!). This work[5] represented an important landmark in showing that a high fibre, high carbohydrate diet could have benefits for diabetic control, but the exact mechanism must remain obscure. The beans may have contributed significant amounts of amylase inhibitors, and in the light of subsequent work, the enormous intake of dietary fibre (96 g/day) seems likely to have provided only a modest contribution to the overall improvements in fasting plasma glucose (− 15%) and cholesterol (− 14%).

It is therefore suggested in this paper that dietary fibre probably does have beneficial effects on glycaemic and lipid control in diabetes, but the effects of dietary fibre alone are fairly small. The small size of its effect in isolation has made it hard to demonstrate convincingly, given the constraints of metabolic studies. Such research has to be meticulously designed and conducted, with close attention to confounding factors like imperfect energy balance (which can affect results even before weight change is detectable).[6] Research which fails to demonstrate an effect needs careful scrutiny of power of the study design to prove 'no effect'.[7] Possible benefits of fibre are shown in Table 2.

With regard to long term dietary management, the actions of dietary fibre cannot be considered meaningfully outside the context of a diet relatively high in carbohydrate and low in fat. In relation to current dietary recommendations for diabetes, the popular term 'high-fibre diet' has been misleading by directing attention away from these other important components of the recommendations.[8]

Does dietary fibre reduce blood glucose?

The first thing diabetologists think about is whether blood glucose is improved or not (sometimes losing sight of the question of whether or not the patient will derive any benefit as a consequence). The evidence is quite convincing that diets high in dietary fibre can improve glycaemic control in both IDDM and NIDDM.[5,9,10,11] Supplementation studies indicate that the dietary fibre component of these diets is indeed having an effect.[12,13,11] Several theories have been raised in explanation. It is possible that insoluble (cereal) and soluble dietary fibre operate in different ways. The effect on blood glucose of cereal fibre, which accelerates gut transit, is perhaps most marked on fasting blood glucose.[9] Soluble fibre such as guar delays gut transit and appears to have less effect on fasting blood glucose, more on post-prandial responses.[13] These actions indicate that dietary fibre cannot be operating simply through delayed post-prandial nutrient absorption. Nor is it entirely the result of delayed gastric emptying, since there is still an effect in gastrectomised patients.[14] The increased gut microbial content may be a factor, and there may be a hormonally mediated action, to reduce gluconeogenesis or hepatic glycogenolysis.

In parallel with reduced blood glucose, dietary fibre leads to reduced plasma insulin[5,13,15] indicating improved insulin sensitivity. Again, under certain conditions the effect of dietary fibre may be small in relation to that of other related diet components. How dietary fibre might improve insulin sensitivity is largely conjectural, but it must depend on actions outside the bowel itself and may relate to volatile fatty acid production. Some sources of dietary fibre are almost completely fermented by anaerobic bowel bacteria, the caecum acting in a fashion similar to a rumen. Additionally, in association with high intakes of dietary fibre, variable amounts of starch can escape digestion in the small bowel to provide a further source for fermentation. The fermentation products, mainly hydrogen and volatile fatty acids (acetate and to a lesser degree propionate and butyrate) are well absorbed to provide about 3 kcal/g carbohydrate in amounts up to 5–10% of total energy on a normal UK diet,

TABLE 3.

Volatile fatty acids from the UK diet[17]

Each g CHO is fermented to 10 mmol VFA
Estimate 40 g/day, i.e. 400 mmol VFA
Energy value at 3 kcal/g 120 kcal/day i.e. 5% total EE

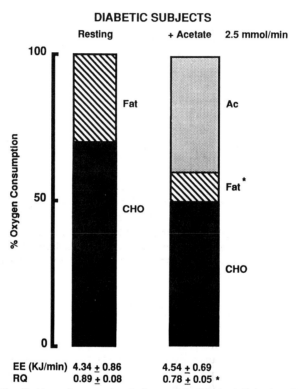

DIABETIC SUBJECTS

Figure 1. Redistribution of energy supply for metabolism in 6 diabetic subjects infused with intravenous sodium acetate at 2.5 mmol/minute (adapted from Akanji et al.[19]).

probably much more on a high fibre diet.[16,17] Butyrate and propionate are utilised in the gut mucosa and removed by the liver on the first pass, but acetate appears in the peripheral circulation in concentrations of 2–3 mmol/l after meals, equivalent to an intravenous infusion rate of 4 mmol/kg/hour.[18] The possible importance of this to diabetes management is that acetate provides an alternative energy substrate to glucose, without requiring insulin secretion[19] (Figure 1). Volatile fatty acids may have additional actions on the endocrine systems governing carbohydrate metabolism.

Does dietary fibre reduce hypoglycaemia?

This is the most critical question asked about treatment by patients receiving insulin and is ignored by diabetologists at their peril.

The smoother profile of blood glucose associated with high dietary fibre intake would suggest the possibility that hypoglycaemic episodes might be reduced, or that a gentler decline in blood glucose should give longer for patients to take corrective action. On the other hand, any treatment which leads to an overall reduction in blood glucose is liable to be associated with more frequent hypoglycaemia, at least of mild hypoglycaemia, and this may be the case with high fibre, high carbohydrate diets.[20] The increased insulin sensitivity with more dietary fibre might also suggest a greater risk of hypoglycaemia from exogenous insulin.

The only study which has addressed the question of hypoglycaemia specifically seems to be in patients who are not diabetic, but are prone to hypoglycaemia dumping following gastrectomy. In this situation galactomannan (a soluble fibre similar to guar) was effective in preventing the post-prandial hypoglycaemic part of the 'lag-storage' type blood glucose curve.[14] The mechanism probably relates to increased viscosity of gut contents, slower transit and possibly altered gut hormone secretion. A similar effect is likely to apply in patients with diabetes.

An intriguing theoretical possibility is that a high dietary fibre intake might be protective against the effects of hypoglycaemia by elevating blood acetate concentration to provide an insulin-independent energy substrate for brain metabolism. There seem to be some patients who apparently function quite adequately despite reporting blood glucose well into the hypoglycaemic range, and it seems possible that the symptoms and dangers of hypoglycaemia could be prevented by the presence of an alternative substrate.

Does dietary fibre delay large vessel disease?
Does it improve blood lipids?

The major long term health risk and the early killer of diabetic patients is accelerated ischaemic vascular disease, and its pathogenesis is probably similar to that in the general population. The main biochemical correlates are elevated blood cholesterol (especially VLDL and LDL) reduced HDL cholesterol, with elevated serum triglycerides possibly playing a special role in NIDDM.

In considering the effects of dietary fibre it is vitally important to differentiate between cereal fibre (practically zero effect) and soluble or viscous fibre sources which appear to have a modestly beneficial effect on all the lipoprotein risk factors for large vessel disease.[5,11,10,13] Total cholesterol is reduced, principally by effects on LDL fractions, also by increased excretion of bile salts, secondary increase in bile acid synthesis from cholesterol and up-regulated hepatic apoprotein B receptors.

The effects of dietary fibre on VLDL or triglycerides are disputed. The improvements found by some groups[5,10] but not by others[21,13] suggest that the diet related improvements are likely to be more related to changes in dietary fat and other constituents. Riccardi *et al.*[10] however, clarified the situation to some degree by demonstrating that increasing dietary carbohydrate (with lower total fat) causes elevated serum VLDL in NIDDM patients, but leguminous dietary fibre opposes this effect.

Does dietary fibre reduce microvascular complications of diabetes?

The answer is an indirect and speculative 'maybe'! By contributing to a general reduction in hyperglycaemia, dietary fibre could claim some of the honours in any consequent fall in microvascular complications, but few diabetologists would find this a convincing argument. Another somewhat tortuous possibility is that the acetate produced by dietary fibre fermentation (see above) could conceivably play a role. It was known for many years that hypophysectomy can arrest the progress of diabetic retinopathy, and diabetes, particularly diabetic retinopathy,[22] is now known to be associated with elevated serum growth hormone which is of course removed by hypophysectomy. Acetate infusion has recently been shown to suppress growth hormone secretion.[19,23] A potential mechanism thus may exist, but much patient observation will be required to prove that dietary fibre has any bearing on the rate of diabetic microvascular complications.

CONCLUSIONS

Putting advice into practice in the 1990s

Dietary fibre on its own as a supplement is of rather limited practical value, even with the more palatable modern administration,[13] although it can improve blood glucose and lipids. It is difficult to be confident about the specific impact on diabetes of dietary fibre as part of a high carbohydrate, high fibre, low fat, diet, but this approach still seems the best starting point as recommended by major national and international bodies.[24,25] Recommendation for the 1990s will probably err more towards the Mediterranean-style diets with greater emphasis on monounsaturated fats and fatty fish, retaining advice to take 30–40 g/d of dietary fibre but specifying perhaps half of this to be soluble, viscous or leguminous in origin. Some of the newer food components with dietary fibre-like activity will also need to be addressed.

Because of problems with palatability and acceptability in the past, greater emphasis is required on the educational or persuasional tactics of the physician-dietitian team. One of the few long term studies of dietary advice in NIDDM[9,15] concludes that body weight and serum triglycerides can both be reduced 1 year after nutrition education, but no differences in nutrient intake could be detected so the fall in body weight was probably the only lasting effect. Several other studies have reported that only very modest alterations in most nutrient intakes can be achieved. Increases in dietary fibre intake of the order 15–20 g/d seem to be possible, however, albeit mostly from cereal sources.[26] This is evidently insufficient by itself to improve diabetic control, as to be expected from controlled metabolic studies.[11] There are immense problems in designing and evaluating nutrition education programmes (Table 2), and generations of dietitians have neglected the need for a proper audit of their activities. The recent emphasis on clinical audit in scientific journals and in the government White Paper[27] should help to catalyse such work in the UK. It seems likely that any recommendation to alter usual eating habits must take account of, firstly, the current behaviour of the target group, and secondly, ways to achieve the goals within the range of eating patterns which are familiar and potentially acceptable.[28] Extensive and high quality dietary survey work is therefore necessary before designing and implementing educational material. Only when programmes are well designed along these lines can the theoretical metabolic improvements be expected.

REFERENCES

1 Trowell H C. Dietary fibre hypothesis of the aetiology of diabetes mellitus. *Diabetes* 1975;**24**:762–5.
2 Kuratsune M, Honda T, Englyst H N, Cummings J H. Dietary fibre in the Japanese diet. *Jap J Cancer Res* 1986;**77**:736–8.
3 Bhatnagar D. Glucose tolerance in North Indians taking a high fibre diet. *Eur J Clin Nutr* 1988;**42**:1023–8.
4 West K M. Epidemiology of diabetes and its vascular lesions. New York: Elsevier, 1978.
5 Simpson H C R, Simpson R W, Lousley S, Carter R D, Geekie M, Hockaday T D R, Mann J I. A high carbohydrate leguminous fibre diet improves all aspects of diabetic control. *Lancet* 1981;**i**:1–5.
6 Lean M E J. Achieving energy balance in clinical studies. *Proc Nutr Soc* 1988;**47**: 65A.
7 Lean M E J, Tennison B R. Dietary fibre, diabetes mellitus and statistics. *Br Med J* 1988;**296**:1797–8.
8 Lean M E J. Diets of dietitians: fatal advice? *Hum Nutr Dietetics* 1988;**1**:223–4.
9 Karlstrom B. Dietary treatment of type 2 diabetes mellitus. *Acta Univ Ups* 1988; **153**:1–50.
10 Riccardi G, Rivellese A, Pacioni D, Genovese S, Mastranzo P, Mancini M. Separate influence of dietary carbohydrate and fibre on the metabolic control in diabetes. *Diabetologia* 1984;**26**:116–21.
11 Vinik A I, Jenkins D J A. Dietary fibre in the management of diabetes. *Diabetes Care* 1988;**11**:160–73.
12 Jenkins D J A, Wolever T M S, Nineham R, Sarson D L, Bloom S R, Ahern J, Alberti K G M M, Hockaday T D R. Improved glucose tolerance four hours after taking guar with glucose. *Diabetologia* 1980;**19**:21–4.
13 Fuessl H S, Williams G, Adrian T E, Bloom S R. Guar sprinkled on food: effect on glycaemic control, plasma lipids and gut hormones in non-insulin dependent diabetic patients. *Diabetic Med* 1987;**4**:463–8.
14 Hopman W P M, Houben P G M P, Speth P A J, Lamers C B H W. Glucomannan prevents postprandial hypoglycaemia in patients with previous gastric surgery. *Gut* 1988;**29**:930–4.

15 Karlstrom B, Vessby B, Asp N G, Ytterfors A. Effects of four meals with different kinds of dietary fibre on glucose metabolism in healthy subjects and non-insulin-dependent diabetic patients. *Eur J Clin Nutr* 1988;**42**:519–26.
16 Cummings J H. Short chain fatty acids in the human colon. *Gut* 1981;**22**:763–79.
17 Cummings J H. Fermentation in the large intestine: evidence and implications for health. *Lancet* 1983;**i**:1206–9.
18 Paterson J L, Barnard M, Frost G, Bloom S R. The effect of acetate on glucose and insulin metabolism. *Diabetic Med* 1989;**6**(2):4A (Abstract).
19 Akanji A O, Bruce M A, Frayn K N. Effect of acetate infusion on energy expenditure and substrate oxidation rates in non-diabetic and diabetic subjects. *Eur J Clin Nutr* 1989;**43**:107–15.
20 Kinmonth, A-L, Angus R M, Jenkins P A, Smith M A, Baum J D. Whole foods and increased dietary fibre improve blood glucose control in diabetic children. *Arch Dis Child* 1982;**57**:187–94.
21 Hollenbeck C B, Coulston A M, Reaven G M. To what extent does increased dietary fibre improve glucose and lipid metabolism in patients with noninsulin-dependent diabetes mellitus (NIDDM)? *Am J Clin Nutr* 1986;**43**:16–24.
22 Sharp *et al.* Growth hormone response to hyperinsulinaemia in insulin-dependent diabetics. Comparison of patients with and without retinopathy. *Diabetic Med* 1984;**1**:55–8.
23 Orskov H, Hansen A P, Hansen H E, Alberti K G M M, Noy G A, Nosadini R. Acetate: inhibitor of growth hormone hypersecretion in diabetic and non-diabetic uraemic subjects. *Acta Endocrinol* 1982;**99**:551–8.
24 American Diabetes Association. Nutritional recommendations and principles for individuals with diabetes mellitus. *Diabetes Care* 1986;**10**:126–32.
25 EASD Diabetes and Nutrition Study Group. Nutritional recommendations for individuals with diabetes mellitus. *Diabetic Nutr Metab* 1988;**1**:145–9.
26 McCulloch D K, Mitchell R D, Ambler J, Tatersall R B. A prospective comparison of 'conventional' and high carbohydrate/high fibre/low fat diets in adults with established Type 1 (insulin-dependent) diabetes. *Diabetologia* 1985;**28**:208–12.
27 Secretary of State for Health. Working for patients. London: HMSO, 1989.
28 Anderson A S, Shepherd R. Beliefs and attitudes toward healthier eating among women attending a maternity hospital. *Proc Nutr Soc* 1990; (in press).

DISCUSSION

Prof Bloom As a diabetologist I tend to use high fibre diets as a really excellent placebo when they say, 'Doctor, can't you do anything'?, rather than spending 4 days explaining that actually I cannot.

Dr Lean At least that sounds less confusing for everyone than if you measured 25 functionless peptide hormones!

Audience Do you think that lente carbohydrate is a useful concept in stopping hypoglycaemic attacks in the middle of the night? Would guar and Horlicks last thing at night protect against them?

Dr Lean I do not know of any hard evidence although we do it, and most diabetologists would recommend something along those lines. The concept of lente carbohydrates is I think here to stay, and the idea of the glycaemic index as a way of assessing the metabolic effects of food, at least in relation to plasma glucose, is being refined gradually. Dietary fibre is one element of the glycaemic index of food.

Audience   You mentioned that high fibre diet is only going to increase lower blood glucose if taken with a high carbohydrate diet. What if some of the carbohydrate is simple sugars?

Dr Lean   Sucrose is a food with a rather low glycaemic index, which some people recommend and some people think of as poison for diabetics. The consensus is that a diet which contains a modest amount of sucrose is perfectly compatible with good diabetic control. We have no grounds for banning it altogether, and a ban would give a whole series of sociological and psychological blows to our patients. The effect of dietary fibre certainly modifies the glycaemic response to sucrose.

Prof Marks   I have suggested that there is no such thing as a diabetic diet. A good diet for diabetics is a good diet for everybody else and vice versa.

Dr Lean   Yes, most of us are potential diabetics and I would agree with you. The diet that we are recommending for people with diabetes is really no different from what we are recommending for everybody who wishes to follow a health-promoting diet.

Prof Marks   A corollary of that is that foods labelled as good for diabetics or prepared especially for diabetics are really now anachronistic.

Dr Lean   There has been a powerful move to have their advertising banned from diabetic journals altogether because there is no evidence that they are having any benefit. In some countries that has already happened. However, in other countries they are still working towards even more special diabetic foods. There are new foods, such as those containing modified starches which are in the pipeline, and may have metabolic advantages; but they have not been tested out on diabetics yet. So it is possible that we are going to see a second generation of diabetic foods, which may in fact have some specific advantage.

Prof Bloom   No diabetic diet, sugar is good for you, diabetic foods are a waste of time, anything else?

Dr Lean   If you are asking, 'What are the recommendations for diabetic diets in the 1990s going to say about dietary fibre?', I think they are not going to be very different from what we have said in the past, but it will be much more clearly specified that we are talking about soluble fibre rather than cereal fibre; they both have a role. We would still like people to take roughly twice the average population fibre consumption, increasing from the high teens into the 30's (grams).

Prof Bloom   Dr Lean, as we said earlier, we recommend very large changes of diet to a very large number of people without testing the consequences. This is against all the basic principles of modern pharmaceutical science, that you should never give a drug until it has been tested properly and all the side effects have been worked out. How do you know that this is not causing Alzheimer's Disease?

Dr Lean   There are groups in the population who take a high fibre diet. Vegetarians and Seventh Day adventists have been studied and there does not seem to be any evidence that they are doing anything very harmful. The question of whether we may be modifying micro-nutrients or absorption of minerals keeps getting raised, but I think the answer is that it does not appear to be having any major effect. Even in the drug world we do not know what the result of taking cimetidine for 30 years will be.

FIBRE AND HYPERCHOLESTEROLAEMIA

Anthony R Leeds
King's College London

ABSTRACT

Recent evidence that aggressive treatment of Hyperlipidaemias, especially Hypercholesterolaemia, can reduce the risk of Coronary Heart Disease, gives new significance to the evidence that foods high in Water-Soluble Dietary Fibre and purified forms of Water-Soluble DF can reduce blood cholesterol. However, almost all studies have been short term (less than 3 months) and there is some doubt that reduced plasma cholesterol levels seen in the short term can be sustained in the long term. Dosage may also be important: studies on very large numbers of subjects may be needed to demonstrate significant changes in blood lipids when small doses of fibre are used. It must also be remembered that some high fibre foods have other characteristics which make them desirable components of a lipid-lowering diet: the composition of the fat and the amino-acid pattern of the protein may be important.

It is probably not unreasonable to advocate the moderate use of high soluble fibre foods (oats, rye, possibly barley, legume seeds) as part of a lipid-lowering diet, though more large scale, longer term studies are needed.

GENERAL DISCUSSION—PM

Prof Bloom   I am much happier with the idea of trying to help a hyper-cholesterolaemic individual who is going to have a heart attack or a stroke than of advising the entire population to eat high bran fibre foods.

Dr Leeds   It is important to remember that there might be side effects of those general recommendations. Those colour slides are of products in New Zealand, where gastroenterologists are increasingly seeing patients with GI symptoms which can be alleviated by reducing consumption of oat bran that has been taken as a result of the publicity.

Audience   Does one treat familial hypercholesterolaemia with diet?

Dr Leeds   On its own, no. Currently you begin with dietary therapy, but to get really good blood profiles you almost invariably need to use drugs.

Audience   I think Gold and Davidson published a study last year where even smaller doses of oat bran gave significant reductions in cholesterol; that is 17 grams of oat bran a day on normal subjects.

Dr Morgan   Guar gum is relatively as effective in hypercholesterolaemics as in normal subjects. In hypercholesterolaemic subjects reductions of up to 30% have been claimed with oats, and in the normal population the reduction seems to be very much smaller. Is there something different going on here, or is it just a question of experimental design?

Dr Leeds   Experimental design is important because we do not have enough studies with appropriate numbers to know exactly what is happening. We are not just interested in fibre. There are other features of oats which may have lipid lowering effects, and which may also have benefits unrelated to lipids, for ischaemic heart disease. Obviously the lipid profile and possibly even the profile of the amino acids in the protein may be beneficial, and that might account for those apparent differences.

Prof Bloom   What do you think about the fact that the viscous fibre has got to be mixed with the food, rather than drunk in tablet form separately? We did a trial of food, in which the tablets were taken with water separately as directed, or the fibre was sprinkled on food. We only saw an effect when it was mixed with food.

Dr Leeds   Perhaps it would also depend on the timing.

Prof Bloom   It does illustrate that other things come into it.

Audience   I understand that Burr's study, which you referred to, involved people who already had some evidence of a coronary event or were very strongly at risk. Those people would have advanced atherosclerosis and one would not expect much regression of that kind of condition. Would these diets not have been aimed at preventing the final event, thrombosis, with which fibre is unconnected?

Dr Leeds All of the patients who participated had just had an acute myocardial infarction, usually about 40 days before entering the trial. So, yes, it is a secondary prevention situation. It is unreasonable to expect fibre to have an effect in a 2 year period in such patients with extensive atherosclerosis, and you would expect it to be much more important in terms of the clinical manifestation, effects on blood lipids, than on thrombosis. Drug trials have shown some degree of slowing down or even regression of atherosclerosis. But the dramatic changes seen with drugs cannot be reproduced with dietary changes. I showed it simply because it is the only trial which really tries to sort out fibre from other factors.

Audience The reduction you get in serum cholesterol with guar gum and bran is actually quite low, 5%. What is the biological significance of that?

Dr Leeds All I can do is quote people like Grundy who on the basis of analysis of all of the dietary trials and also some drug trials are able to say that a 1% reduction in total cholesterol seems to lead to a 2% reduction in coronary heart disease risk or mortality risk. It does not necessarily follow that you can extrapolate that to effects achieved by fibre.

LIST OF DELEGATES
FIBRE – IS IT GOOD FOR YOU?

Allen E P
London

Ambasna C
London

Anderson A O
Guildford

Armstrong H
Birmingham

Barbosa M C de A
Reading

Barker E S
Surrey

Barnard M
London

Barton S J
Surrey

Bell S M
Welwyn G City

Bernett J
London

Bird M J
Surrey

Blanchflower S J
Isleworth

Brown P J
London

Bower D E
Dartford

Bowey E A
London

Boyd E J S
Middlesex

Brough S H
Leicestershire

Buttriss J
London

Byrne A
London

Clarke D N
Stirling

Clowes R M
London

Costa N M B
Reading

Crocker A
Gravesend

Dabai F D
Reading

Dickens W E
Havant

Dickie N H
London

Dihmis P A
London

Elhardallou S B
Reading

Frost G
W Sussex

Gatenby S J
Guildford

Gott C L
St Albans

Hardcastle D M
London

Hashmi S Z A
Braintree

Hawkins N
London

Horton T J
London

Houghan A
London

Jones P M
Chelmsford

Judd P A
London

Lund E K
Norwich

MacLeod J
London

Mahdi G S
London

Majumdar S K
Dartford

Malkin J C
London

Mason P
London

McMillan K
Milton Keynes

Middleton H
Hereford

Missen A J
London

Montgomery R D
Birmingham

Moore F J
Guildford

Morris J
London

O'Donnell M G
London

Peebles S A
Southampton

Petley H
Guildford

Pozsonyi A E
London

Prinja H Brentford	Snow A Dartford	Walker L A Reading
Reid K Croydon	Sussmann K London	Waller E G London
Reilly H Birmingham	Sutherland K W Colchester	Warren R Ashford
Riordan A M Cambridge	Symonds D Norwich	Whadcoat J London
Robshaw J E Bournemouth	Taylor E J Loughborough	Wisbey R Huntingdon
Rowland I Surrey	Travis J S Guildford	Wise A Aberdeen
Sender S N London	Tredger J Guildford	Yates C London
Sinfield L J Leicester	Tuffrey V London	
Skypala I London	Walker A F Reading	

MEDICAL RELATIONS PUBLICATIONS

CURRENT APPROACHES SERIES

Vertigo   (reprint October 1985)

Small Bowel Disease

Endometrial Carcinoma

Risk/Benefits of Antidepressants

Affective Disorders in the Elderly

Childbirth as a Life Event

Sleep Disorders

Advances in Pancreatitis

Sudden Cardiac Death

Neuropsychiatric Aspects of AIDS

Stress, Immunity and Disease

The Problem of Recurrent Abdominal Pain

Breaking Bad News

Mental Retardation

Panic—Symptom or Disorder

The above publications can be obtained by writing to:

DUPHAR MEDICAL RELATIONS
Duphar Laboratories Limited
West End
Southampton
SO3 3JD